GUERRILLA
PUBLISHING

Revolutionary Book Marketing Strategies
to Make Your First $1000 on Kindle

advertising ★ release strategies ★ pricing & preorders ★ press
coverage ★ book giveaways ★ targeted readership ★ viral exposure

DEREK MURPHY, PH.D.

Join the <u>Guerrilla Publishing Facebook group</u> for
community + accountability + support!

www.creativindie.com/GP

CONTENTS

PREFACE

TRAIN THE INTERNET TO SELL BOOKS FOR YOU

So many books are being published each year, it's hard to stand out and get your book noticed. And it may seem like you're up against impossible odds. After all, traditional publishers spend hundreds of thousands of dollars on a book launch and get blurbs by famous authors. They have websites that get a ton of traffic and huge email lists. How can you possibly compete? Even worse, you've heard of other "authors" completely gaming the system, making tens of thousands of dollars by tricking readers into buying crappy books stuffed with free content or translated garbage.

In the face of all this, it's easy to get frustrated and say something like, "well screw all of that noise. Marketing is a joke, so I'm just going to keep writing instead." You may even hear other self-publishing authors say that it's *better* to do things professionally even if that doesn't translate into book sales. So they focus on their writing and mimic the book marketing of traditionally published authors.

The problem is, even if you navigate self-publishing successfully and are able to get a great book cover; even if you get a decent website up and figure out your email list, optins and autoresponders, even if you do *everything* right – it's still not nearly enough to compete.

You're trying to play the game by the rules set by the publishing industry. Meanwhile, if you're traditionally published, things can be even more frustrating. You may not have control over your own book files, pricing or Amazon page. You may assume the publishing company is going to promote or market your book, but in many cases – *they don't.* That can leave traditionally published authors scrambling to build their own author platform and boost sales so that their publishing contract doesn't get dropped.

Unfortunately, since most authors want their books to sell, but have no idea how to make that happen, they copy what other indie authors are doing online – spamming Twitter and Facebook. Posting their book launches in other people's groups. Getting people to like their Facebook author pages or vote for their book covers in some contest. *Stuff that doesn't work.*

I'm writing this book to convince you to **stop playing by the rules.** The game is rigged. You need to think outside the box and find new and exciting ways to connect with your readers directly. You need to find ways to get the media talking about you and sharing your content. You need to find ways to connect with other authors in your genre.

A few years ago I wrote *Book Marketing is Dead*, the main point of which was: stop being annoying and telling everybody about your book. Find indirect, long term marketing strategies that center on building an author brand and platform. Since then I've started publishing my own fiction and have been able to experiment with all kinds of book promotion.

This is a crash course on some of the more creative book marketing strategies I've discovered, in my first year of publishing fiction (I reached $3000 in profit a month in the third month). It builds on a lot of the content marketing and platform building tactics I've used to build two six-figure businesses around my non-fiction books. People often say it's harder to market fiction; I've found it to be easier, because there is so much less competition (there are tons of books, but very few authors are using the strategies I'm using to get visibility and reach new readers).

Although I've gone through all the stages of publishing and marketing a bestseller, this is not a *complete* guide to every single option out there. I'm only going to mention the things I actually use, that I know work, and ignore all the other things that don't get results. We'll discuss paid advertising, release strategies, pricing and preorders, book giveaways, how to target your audience, viral exposure and press coverage, marketing hacks, and how to reach your first $1000 on Kindle.

These methods may not work forever, but that's part of the beauty: indie authors have the unique ability to publish quickly and be flexible with their marketing strategy. We have the freedom to do whatever we want with our own books, and test things out to make sure we're making as much money as possible with our content (you may not think money is the right goal for authors, but it's an easy benchmark of how many readers are enjoying your books, and all authors should care about having a larger impact with their work).

QUIT MARKETING AND FOCUS ON WRITING

The main thing I want to stress in this book is that indie authors should not be focusing on the slow, long-term stuff that traditional publishers use to sell books (like sending out review copies three months early or getting into bookstores). Indie authors should be using our natural strengths—speed and agility—to take advantage of resources and outlets that traditional publishers don't have access to.

This isn't a book about flash in the pan marketing, promising huge results. It's a book about publishing *quickly* and quietly launching a #1 bestseller without a lot of fuss. So you can spend less time marketing, and more time writing. This is a book of simple, practical (and yet genius) tricks that will make readers love you, bring in lots of traffic, and keep your books visible long term.

INTRODUCTION

LAUNCH BIG EVEN IF YOU'RE STARTING SMALL

For the past ten years I've been helping authors publish and market their books. First I figured out how to build an online platform. Then I learned book design and formatting, setting up an author website, positioning your book to sell on Amazon or other ebook retailers, and getting enough visibility for people to buy it. Usually when I coach clients, I'll want them to set up *everything* the right way, because it all helps a little bit. There are so many variables in an author platform, and if you do something wrong you could be losing 80% of your sales without ever knowing why. You need to *plug the leaks* before you start marketing your books, or you'll be throwing money away. However, most authors aren't equipped to do everything right on their own; and many authors can't afford to spend thousands of dollars paying an expert to do it for them.

The result is that the majority of authors have haphazard, confusing online presences which do next to nothing to sell their books. This is evidenced by the common frustration many authors experience when, after all their hard work, their book isn't selling. *Anywhere.*

It's easy to become invisible online, and difficult to stay on top of the bestseller lists where your books can actually get seen. That's why, when I started publishing my own fiction this year, I wanted to build a stable online presence that attracts readers on autopilot. However, the better I got at book marketing and launching a new title, the more I realized exactly what elements were *crucial* to the success of a book, and what elements weren't.

Since one of the common complaints I hear from authors is that they hate spending time marketing their books when they'd rather be writing, in this book I will focus on the 5% of book marketing "hacks" I've been using this year to make my books bestsellers with very little time or money spent.

Because the truth is, you can launch a book without being on social media, without advertising and promotion, without an author website, and still be successful. As long as you know how to use a few tools really well (better than everyone else). The easiest way to fail is to try to do everything you hear about – every new gadget and strategy and platform. That's the *shotgun* approach to marketing, or the "shot in the dark." It's basically, "I have no idea what I'm doing, and nothing is working anyway, so I might as well try everything."

The purpose of this book is for you to avoid ever feeling that way, by providing simple, actionable, measurable steps to publishing a high quality book quickly, doing only as much marketing as is necessary to launch your book professionally, and keep it selling enough to support you while you write another.

WHO AM I AND WHY YOU SHOULD LISTEN TO ME?

My name is Derek Murphy. I have a PhD in Literature and was recently featured on CNN for holding a writing retreat in a castle. After spending nearly a decade as a struggling artist and writer, I shifted my focus away from "following my passion" to "providing value." Now I make a living publishing books, which lets my wife and I travel full-time. I've written about 15 books. My first was a disaster—I did everything wrong, and then some. I had no idea how to promote or market it. Since then, as an editor, book designer and marketer, I've helped over a thousand authors publish and launch their own books, and helped create dozens of bestsellers.

For several years I've been blogging about all the new book marketing strategies I've discovered on my site CreativIndie. Recently I started making videos as well, and have over 400,000 views on YouTube, mostly for my in-depth formatting and cover design tutorials. In 2016 I started publishing fiction, and after less than a year, I'm earning enough in book sales to write full time. I did that by building a big platform and an email list of 25,000 readers before I published my first novel. I took what I learned and put it into a course on book marketing, which sold out on launch (due mostly to the list of 35,000 authors I've built over the past five years by giving away free resources).

Now when I publish a new book, *I know it will sell well*. I don't have to worry about things like making money with my fiction, building a platform, getting book reviews, setting up a website and getting traffic, getting PR and media attention— most of that stuff is built into the author platform I set up earlier this year. So now I'm just focused on writing more books, because every book I publish boosts my income.

I'm always looking for ways to get bigger results with less effort, so I avoid anything that takes too much time, energy or money unless I can see significant results. I'm willing to test things out though—and it's not that all those things I skip don't work. It's just that I don't need them, because I'm found better things—things most authors aren't using at all.

As I write this, I'm working on a partner course called the *21 Day Bestselling Author Platform*. It's about building a solid platform that is essential for a long term author career. But some authors don't want to spend three weeks setting all that stuff up. And while I have tons of publishing resources, I didn't have a simple, practical, in-depth, all-in-one place guide to publishing, book design, and launching a book as quickly and easily as possible (and doing it better than the 95% of the self-published authors who never make a profit from their books).

So this is it. It's called *Guerrilla Publishing*, because I'm not playing by the rulebook. I don't care how the publishing industry thinks or what the gatekeepers are thinking. My own goal is to find readers of my genre and turn them into raving fans by over-delivering on their expectations and giving them a satisfying reading experience.

Guerrilla is a style of warfare intended to surprise and harass enemies. It can also mean using unconventional and usually inexpensive means to generate interest or raise concern among the public. That's basically how I'll use it: book marketing strategies from the trenches to help you win the publishing war. However, instead of "surprise and harass" I will focus on "surprise and delight." First you need to show up and get in front of the right people. Then you need to surprise and delight them. You need to be remarkable enough to be noticed. This is actually, far easier than you'd think.

For example, rather than creating a huge self-publishing resource, I can share an animated gif of a cat pounding on a keyboard with a clever caption, and it will get 10x the reach. The less you're trying to sell, the easier it will be to reach people. When you're trying to sell something, or get people to take action, when you want them to sign up/buy/download, that's when it's hard. But you shouldn't be trying to do that! At least not to strangers.

Think of it like *Duck Duck Goose*. You can't just yell "goose!" to the first person you meet and expect them to chase after you. You need people to be involved first, sitting in a circle, with a shared understanding of the game. They need to be invested. They have to want to play. Then you need to say "duck" several times... you build up the tension. You make people want it, but you don't give it to them. Then, finally, when you say "goose" they are fully committed. They want in. They jump up and follow after you. That's what we're going for.

My goal in this book is to hit everything essential to publishing and launching a book, while skipping everything else. I won't necessarily explain or justify in great detail *why* I've made the choices I have, why one platform is better than the others, why I don't do this or that. You can take my word for it, or you can spend years painstakingly researching the same things I've learned after doing this for over a decade. Knowledge is only power if it helps you achieve your goals. Too much knowledge can be distracting and debilitating. I want to help you finish, publish and launch your book without sinking in the quagmire of TMI (too much information). That said, take imperfect action and see what happens. If it's not working, do something else.

What follows is a brief outline of topics. I'm assuming you're starting with zero platform and want to launch to #1 bestseller and continue selling books after that. I'm also assuming you want to make more money than you spend. You may feel like money is irrelevant – it isn't. Money is an easy indicator of how much value you're putting out into the world. If you aren't focused on writing books that readers enjoy, you're going to have a difficult time trying to make a living with your writing. In the first section of this book, *Preparation*, I talk about the importance of writing the kind of book that readers love, because the type of book you write will have the largest impact on whether or not you can make a living with your writing. But if you've finished your book already and just need some guerrilla marketing strategies, you can skip to some of the more detailed topics in the *Publishing* or *Launching* sections.

You can publish as cheaply as you want to, or pay for expert publishing services. You can save money by doing things yourself, but having a homemade cover, formatting and website could really hurt your book launch. So at the very least, try and get some professional feedback. You can get some help and support by joining my free Facebook group, Guerrilla Publishing. I really want to make this book valuable for you, so I also set up a free 5-Day Challenge, to encourage you to take action and implement some of these strategies while getting personal support.

Finally, while this book will teach you everything you need to know—the bare minimum to launching a bestselling book without getting distracted by all the things you don't really need—actually setting everything up by yourself can be challenging. If you want to shorten the learning curve, you can buy the companion course and learn exactly how I set up my sales funnels and book launches. (I don't let many students in because I need to focus on my own writing, but there are limited spaces available for committed authors).

A word of caution

Guerrilla publishing is about *winning* the publishing war, and by "winning" I mean, being one of the extremely few authors who make more than they spend. So hold yourself accountable. Treat it like a game. Cut down on expenses, focus on the wins. Stay in the green. Don't assume all the money you pump into your book is an investment.

I love thinking up new ways to reach and attract readers, to get them to know who you are. But don't bet the farm on an unproven book. The point of "guerrilla publishing" is *not* to spend lots of money on a big, crazy idea, but to start small and cheap, constantly tweak, pivot quickly and make incremental improvement.

1: PREPARATION

This section is about writing the kind of books that will sell. If you've already finished your book and have no interest in writing something else, or fixing your manuscript to make it more likely to sell, you can skip this section. However, if your book doesn't sell as well as you'd like it to, and you're not sure what's going wrong, it's almost certainly related to this section.

WHAT KIND OF BOOK TO WRITE

This section will be controversial, and that's not my fault. The problem is, the ruling ideology of creative production says that you should *write for yourself.* That "good writing" or "real art" comes from personal inspiration, from inside you, and trying to figure out what the market wants will dilute your pure voice of divined wisdom. But that's a romantic fantasy, and it's the reason most artists and authors never make any money. It's also the *direct opposite* of the *fundamental basics* of business and entrepreneurship. It leads to authors creating "art" and then being confused and frustrated because nobody wants to buy it.

If you're writing literary fiction, or you want to get an agent or publisher, then your books do need to be unique and original. For the majority of popular genres, however, even traditional publishers and agents expect to see all the common writing tropes, the basic building blocks of story structure, and a similarity to books that are already selling.

Sales depend on how many readers will want to buy your book—but *success* depends on how much the book satisfies them. If the book doesn't hit the same emotional buttons they crave and enjoy, the reasons why they read that genre, they won't be satisfied. Some authors *deliberately* avoid all tropes or clichés or conventions and try to make something new and original, something creative that's never been done before. Almost all of the time, that's not what readers want in a book. It's too much work and effort. They want something entertaining and comfortable. You need to give them the experience they're looking for but modify the themes and events so they encounter something exciting and new. If you feel like this is "pandering" or "selling out" I probably can't convince you otherwise.

But you do need to know, going into this publishing business, that you're deliberately breaking the #1 rule of entrepreneurship by trying to sell a product without first asking whether anybody wants it. Your job will be to educate and convince people that your book is *good* or worth reading, even if they just don't enjoy it.

Yes, of course you can write for yourself without thinking of the market and still write a popular bestseller. But it's rare, and you're gambling. Your author career is based on a relationship with your readers: you provide an enjoyable reading experience and they pay you for it. It's *easier* to try and figure out what they want first. You can read the bestsellers in your genre and isolate the common elements, and look at cover designs to see what's selling. Then build a community of readers who enjoy those books and get feedback.

The majority of authors begin by writing what they're passionate about, what they want to write. I did the same thing of course, and had several unsuccessful books before I decided I'd rather make things easy on myself.

WHO READS THAT KIND OF BOOK

If you've already decided you'd like to write some books that more people will buy, by trying to satisfy readers of a certain genre, it's worth figuring out who reads that genre and how many of them there are.

Some genres are harder to write than others; some readers are more demanding. There are also different genre conventions—young adult books tend to be around 65,000 words long, while epic fantasy books are twice that. (Which means, depending on the genre, you'll need to work twice as hard to finish one product.) *Also,* however, I think epic fantasy readers expect better writing, more fancy prose, while young adult books tend to focus more on action and story, and usually use simpler language. You need to learn the rules of the game, which is usually done by reading a lot of books in your genre and trying to create something similar. However it gets more complicated when you consider reader habits: young adult readers often reader several books a month, while epic fantasy readers typically read less. And if you're writing non-fiction business books, adult readers usually only consume a handful of books a year.

In general, write what you want and do the best you can—but if you're not happy with sales or are getting negative reviews, you might want to try another subject or genre where the readers are less picky and go through books at a more rapid rate. One site that collects this kind of information is K-lytics.com. Those reports might not be the foundation of your publishing schedule, but it would be a good idea to check out their reports and get a basic sense of what you can expect from your genre. Other tools I use are KindleSpy and KDPRocket. They let me peek at books or genres on Amazon, find out what people are searching for and what comes up for certain keywords, and also how many sales and downloads books in my genre are getting.

There are three basic steps to a successful book (by successful I mean a book that earns money and readers enjoy). The first is *visibility*. The book has to get seen. The second part is *conversion*: the offer has to be convincing enough to make them want to buy or download it (even a free book can fail if it doesn't convert well). The third is *satisfaction*.

WHERE ARE THEY?

If you know who you're writing for and what kind of people might read your book, and you've written and designed a book that will appeal to them, you're ready for the next step: you need to put your book in front of them and see if they like it.

To get seen, you need to put your book in front of readers where they already are—which means you need to know where they hang out. This includes blogs, websites or social media. I always prefer online spaces where you can reach more people with less money, but the right, highly targeted offline spaces, such as a genre-specific conference, may work as well. We'll talk more about *how* to put your book in front of the right readers later, but for now it's enough to understand getting your book seen is already a big challenge. Most books get put on a blog with no traffic or on Amazon with millions of competing titles. Unless your book rises to the top, either by being a bestseller in its category or showing up in search results, it's invisible. If you don't have your own traffic or platform, you'll need to pay to access someone else's through advertising.

DO THEY REALLY WANT YOUR BOOK?

The second step is *conversion*. You got your book seen by the right readers. But did they buy or download it? Conversion is a process in itself, which usually goes like this: the book shows up. The cover and title captivates their attention, at least enough to get them to read the description. The description sounds like something they'd like to read. They check out a few reviews to make sure the quality will be decent, and finally they'll look at the price (if they want the book enough, the price doesn't matter – but if they're on the fence, a cheap deal might push them over the edge).

The problem many authors face is they *think* they've written a book for a certain type of reader, but actually haven't. They'll look at some other major bestseller like *The Martian*, and write a scifi/space book that is totally different. They'll say "*The Martian* sold a million copies, so even if my book sells only 10% of that, that's still 100,000 copies!"

Even worse, they'll often make critical mistakes with the design of their book, choosing the wrong cover (that looks nothing like the book they think they're competing with) or failing to position it in an attractive way (clearly communicating who the book is for and why they'll love it).

If you wrote a book you think will appeal to a certain genre, but don't actually read books in that genre, or worse, you *dislike* that genre, you might have a problem. Some authors look at a book like *Twilight* or *Shades of Gray* and think, "That book was terrible... so I'll write a vampire romance that's *better* and it will be successful."

If you don't know why a book was successful or what readers liked about it, you can't hope to emulate its success.

The easiest way to check your assumptions is to do some testing. Luckily with Facebook ads you can immediately put your book in front of the right readers and see how they respond. You can test your cover, description and sales copy and see if your book or offer is strong enough to get them to click; and then see how many of those clicks actually continue on to purchase the book. Then you can tweak your cover, description and editorial reviews until your conversion is halfway decent. (If your funnel is broken with a bad cover or description or too few reviews, you'll have to throw much more money at the problem and are unlikely to make a return on the investment).

MAKE SURE YOU TELL A GREAT STORY

The third piece to a successful book is a great story (for fiction). A great story is one that keeps readers reading. If the book is too slow or doesn't feel like it's going anywhere, or isn't the type of book they enjoy, they'll probably stop reading. Good books have an emotional payout, usually at the end, which rewards readers for sticking it through—but some don't and are disappointing. Once they've started reading, you're responsible for their satisfaction. If you can't satisfy them or keep them reading, they'll feel disappointed.

Most major genres of popular fiction have predictable tropes and follow a standard story structure. Romance is an exception, which is more character driven and less formulaic (to a point). Literary non-fiction is another exception, as it's usually more creative and less predictable. It also matters if you're shooting for an agent or publisher, rather than self-publishing. Publishers want something that's unique and fresh, that also satisfies genre expectations. They don't want something too clichéd. But readers are still hungry for the types of books that publishers won't publish (like shifter romance). You need to write the right kind of book for your desired results.

But there are rules to every genre.
Even if the norm is to break all the rules.

Some authors *hate* plotting and formula because they think it makes books boring and predictable, and keep trying to make something totally different. They're creating for the art, because it makes them happy, for themselves. I've had friends get angry at me for suggesting that this is a selfish, lazy way of publishing.

What I meant was, authors who are focused on pleasing readers are more likely to adapt, change and improve their writing to better satisfy (which will lead to more sales with less marketing). Being a successful writer is not the same as being a *good* writer; it only depends on changing your definition of good from "what I enjoy writing" to "what readers enjoy reading." Many authors get frustrated by poor sales and intentionally set out to write "a bad book" full of clichés and tropes... and are exasperated when that one wins awards, gets a publishing deal or becomes a bestseller. But books aren't objectively good or bad. And whether or not you like what you are writing is a personal choice... being frustrated or unhappy about writing books that people want and actually make a living writing is a problem with your fundamental beliefs about creativity conflicting with the basics precepts of business and entrepreneurship. You can't *change* the market, or educate the 100 million readers who love vampire romance novels to appreciate "higher quality" literature. So you can complain about it, or you can embrace it and use your writing skills to make a living by providing reading experiences that people are willing to pay for.

MAKE SURE IT SATISFIES THE RIGHT READERS

There is always some amount of balance between what you're trying to write and what readers enjoy. My advice is, rather than compromising and writing something that you halfway enjoyed writing and readers halfway enjoy reading (which doesn't really help anyone), you should focus on getting better at writing stories readers love and rave about. Write enough of those, build a following, make a steady income, and you can return to the exploratory, innovative books you're more passionate about if you want to.

The only way to make sure your book satisfies readers is to put it out there... but you don't have to put out the whole thing. I've put out the first few chapters on Wattpad, or even published half-books to see what the response was. Some of the methods I've used are controversial, but the idea is this: instead of writing a whole series of novels, I'd rather put out the first few chapters and see if anybody likes it.

Rather than developing a full series that sells moderately well, I planned to put out 10 first installments of potential series to see which was the most popular, and then continue those. My plans have gotten messier since I started publishing, so I'm not doing exactly that, though I'll be doing something pretty close.

I also put those books out as permafree books – which got about 100,000 downloads in 2016. That gives me lots of reviews and feedback (I just switched one of them back to paid, now that it has 178 reviews, and my sales rank is staying pretty strong with little promotion). But you don't have to do it my way. I have friends who just launched at

2.99 and did really well. As long as you keep producing quickly and put out more books, and as long as you are writing in very popular genres, you may do fine. But if *not*, putting a non-selling book on permafree can be easier than spending a lot of time or money trying to sell it.

FIX IT

I was a book editor for several years, while I was working on my MA in Literature. I got pretty good at it. Even so, I routinely miss typos in my own work. And yet, I don't always recommend editing. It's a great idea if you can afford it, especially if it's your first book, as long as you get the right kind of editing. But I don't like seeing it referred to as mandatory.

Lots of indie authors argue that self-published books need to be as professional as traditionally published books, but that's difficult to achieve on a budget and also won't make much difference in the book's success (there are tens of thousands of well-edited self-published books that sell less than 100 copies, and the majority of bestselling, indie published books on Kindle are probably full of errors (often the books launch with typos but then get cleaned up later once they're selling strongly).

Which means two things:
1. Readers don't really care about a few typos and mediocre design, as long as the story entertains them.
2. Editing the words isn't as important as fixing the story.

The problem is, while some copy editors will comment on structure and story architecture, or at least point out flaws in character development, motivation and plot, they generally won't *fix* the story – that's your job. And the story is important.

A great story, poorly written, will sell better than an uninteresting story with beautiful writing (in fact, beautiful writing is usually a distraction from story altogether, in that it points to the author behind it).

When I started writing fiction, *Plot Perfect, Write from the Middle, Story Grid* and *Story Fix* were the books that finally made story "make sense" to me. There are other books on story, and on writing, but many of them are misleading or unhelpful: they focus on the craft of writing and complex issues while skipping basic story architecture.

PLOTTERS & PANTSERS

Personally, I had trouble getting through a whole book until I learned story structure and plotting – and after I learned it I've found it much easier to produce fiction that sells, much more quickly. Which is why I recommend plotting to everyone, especially first time authors who are struggling to finish a book or are writing books that don't get any traction from readers.

Usually, the writing isn't the problem, it's the story. At the same time, I can't say anymore that plotting is better than pantsing. Many authors "write from the seat of their pants" and discover the story as they go. This works fine for romance, and character-driven stories, and *sometimes* can create more exciting developments.

As a vast generalization, in my experience plotters write well-crafted stories that fill in all the plot gaps, and pantsers are strong on action and dialogue, which can make their books gripping but also a little aimless or without direction. I also think it might be possible that pantsers sell better – but only if they're writing in very popular genres.

However, pantsers usually need to spend a lot on an editor, to fill in all the gaps, point out story flaws, and fix grammar and typos (plotters, I think, tend to write slower but end up with a cleaner final copy that doesn't need much revision).

Again, these are simply things I've noticed after working with about a thousand authors, but of course they aren't universal. My point is that, both pantsers and plotters have strengths and weaknesses, and both need to do what's comfortable for them while recognizing the room for improvement.

Recently I've decided to try co-writing with some fast drafters to complement each other's strengths; I can plot and outline, my partner can write a first draft, and I can polish and edit. I know other co-writers who both take turns writing the first draft so they can finish quickly and hand it off to an editor.

My main point though, even if you're writing non-fiction, is to focus on the story first. The big stuff, the organization and theme, the introduction and conclusion. The story of a book, is how the content is processed through a central character that readers care about to make it *matter*. Make sure everything fits together well and makes sense – and do it long before you start paying attention to the individual words on the page.

MAKE IT BETTER

Once you have read a few books on plotting, organization and structure, and made sure your outline is tight and satisfying, and everything is in the right place, then you can began cleaning up the writing.

If you need an editor on a budget, you can try writing groups on Facebook or hiring someone cheap on Fiverr. com. You can pay for the first 10 or 20 pages and see how many typos they catch. Personally, I finish a book and send it to beta readers early, and they'll usually help me pick out the typos before the book is published.

It's difficult to catch all typos – I routinely find them even in traditionally published books – but if there are too many (more than one or two per chapter) they'll be distracting and leave a bad impression on readers. So they are dangerous, because if you publish too soon, you'll earn negative comments about the editing that will stick on your Amazon page forever (even after you've uploaded a revised copy).

So do the best you can; get friends or family to help proofread it. Trade edits with other authors in your genre. If you can afford it, hiring a writing coach or professional editor can help identify your writing weaknesses.

EDITING, SELF-EDITING, HIRING AN EDITOR

Choosing an editor is a big decision and can account for the bulk of your publishing costs. Generally, I would look for someone who has edited books in your genre before;

I would try to get testimonials from other authors, and then check out those books online to see how well they were edited. It also might be worthwhile to hire from UpWork or a community marketplace which has reviews and feedback. Many professional editors have their own websites, so you only see what they want you to see; on the other hand, talented editors usually move away from freelance websites because they can earn more on their own without competing (I set up an editing company, The Book Butchers, which gets a steady stream of work without promotion, mostly by word of mouth.)

If you do have a budget for an editor, have them do a sample first, maybe pay them for the first 10 pages to make sure you're a good fit. Then ask them to comment on the story and big picture issues first, so you can do a little revision if necessary, before going through and proofreading (I think a two-step process like this will be the most valuable for all books, but you may need to negotiate a price with your editor). Generally editing costs about 1 cent per word, but there is a big range. I started at 2 cents per word, but now that I have my PhD I probably wouldn't do it for less than 4 cents a word. Price doesn't necessarily indicate quality; only demand – so there's nothing wrong with going cheaper, though more expensive editors may have more experience.

I wrote a massive post on common writing mistakes, and things to look out for if you're editing your first draft: 25 self-editing tips.

WORKING WITH A WRITING COACH

I'll admit I don't know exactly what a writing coach does. In my defense, there seems to be lots of author-related services popping up with vague titles, so I'm commenting based on what I've seen online but don't actually have first-hand experience with.

In my understanding, a writing coach is like a personal trainer. They'll tell you what to do, how to do it, what needs improving, check in with you to make sure you're working, and may also include publishing services like editing, cover design or help uploading your files.

In many cases, getting support, feedback and accountability can be hugely beneficial to authors, so I see the value. I'm trying to provide the same kind of support and accountability, but with online groups and email series so I don't have to charge several thousand dollars.

Hiring a writing coach to get you to finish the book you've been wanting to write, but never get around to, might be a good idea. However I am reluctant to endorse writing coaches (or small presses) who offer a done-for-you publishing package. From what I've seen online, writing coaches and small presses *may* not have talented in-house designers, which usually means they outsource design.

If I go to a writing coach or small press website and see their example book covers are ugly, that makes me doubt everything they offer: even if they help you finish your book, and include editing, if they can't help you get an amazing cover or know who to sell and market your book, you're shooting yourself in the foot (I also work with authors who sign up with a writing coach or small press, and then hire me for cover design anyway as an added expense – and then they need to get permission from their coach/publisher to use the cover that will sell).

I have lots to say about cover design, which has been my main business for the past ten years, but I'll save it for later. My main point is this: it's tempting to want to hand over control to somebody who knows what they're doing and promises to just take care of everything for you, so you can focus on writing. And sometimes that can totally be worth it – it'll save you a lot of time and self-publishing can be overwhelming.

On the other hand, editing and book design are totally different skills, and you can usually get much better quality for much cheaper if you find the providers and hire them directly. Personally I would hire an accountability coach or a writing coach to help me tell my story, but someone else for the editing, and someone else for cover design. (Actually, however, I just studied plotting and literature for ten years, put a book up on preorder and forced myself to start writing it... figuring out the plot helped a lot, but mostly it was the deadline and determination that got me through the first book).

★ I'm not saying all writing coaches and small presses are bad – only that you need to be careful and do some research. I may actually stop offering cover design and only sell all-inclusive packages, because I hate seeing authors hire me for a cover but then have no idea what to do with it, and I'd rather just do everything myself so I can make sure it's successful.

SETTING REALISTIC EXPECTATIONS AND GOALS

Most authors say something like, "I'm not writing for the money." But then they spend a lot of time, effort and financial resources trying to get people to buy their books. And most of them fail: there's a lot of competition, and many authors think they have a world-changing book that just needs to get on Oprah so it can sell a million copies.

A lot of writing groups are full of support and encouragement, because they know that finishing the book is a huge hurdle and authors need motivation and optimism to see it through. But positive thinking will not help your book sell.

Last year I wrote a post on <u>how much authors really make.</u> In that article, I defined "success" as selling over a thousand copies, which is really hard to do unless you're doing a lot of things right. At the time I wrote the article, there were 4,572,492 ebooks on Kindle, and roughly 10,000 of them were doing pretty well (books in the top 10,000 sell at least 10 copies or so per day. After that, visibility drops and sales dry up). I estimated that only %.000625 of authors are actually selling enough books to make a living.

It's possible that my calculations are way off; there are better sources that track Amazon data like this. My point was that there isn't an "average earnings" for authors because the vast majority of authors lose money publishing. There is no *average*, there is only the *exception*. The authors making money are doing things differently than the majority of writers who are losing money. Which means, the majority of writers and self-publishing gurus who talk about publishing and marketing, even those with big platforms, may not be the best people to listen to.

I want to help you become one of the writers who can build a readership and earn money with your writing, but it has to be a deliberate choice. You need to decide you want to make money with your writing, and write the kind of books that allow you to do that more easily, rather than assume that the marketplace will support whatever kind of books you want to write.

In another article I wrote recently, I called *hubris* the cardinal sin of self-publishing, because many authors assume their books are "better" than the mega-bestsellers in a genre without actually figuring out why those books are so popular. If you think your books are "better written" than *Twilight* or *Three Shades of Gray* and that therefore fans of those books will enthusiastically embrace yours, you've probably missed something (especially if you've never even read those books but just assume they are crap).

It's also dangerous to say, "That book sold 30 million copies, if I sell just 10% as well, I'll be a millionaire." It's important to have big dreams, but the lure of quick riches can cause you to spend $10K thinking it's no big deal because you'll earn it all back.

Instead, I urge you to take some smaller, more practical steps. For almost every book, by a new author with very little platform, I think **100 sales on launch** is a reasonable goal. If you can sell 100 copies in a few days, that will get you up to the first page of your categories on Amazon, where you'll try to stay as long as possible. After that, if you can sell 10 copies a day, you'll stay in the top 10,000. It's not that easy actually, but if you can pull it off you should feel very proud. Once you have several books out and have used some of my tips to build a big platform, some traffic, and an email list, you may want to shoot for more. You'll generally be able to launch better with every new book, so your goals should keep climbing.

I'd like to reach the point where I can get 1000 sales on a launch, and I'm getting pretty close, but half of that is from my platform and half is from ad-stacking (which I'll discuss later). Even so, that might push me up to 500+ sales, and if I've done my premarketing well and made the book "sticky" by training Amazon to sell for me, I can pick up another 500 sales from natural traffic.

DON'T SPEND 5 YEARS WRITING IT

The other piece of advice I usually give to first-time authors is to start with something simple. Most people have *one* book they want to write, and it's one they're passionate about. Something they believe in. They get too involved in the process, get stuck on the early drafts, and spend years without making progress. It's easy to be paralyzed by indecision, and the first book you publish will be the one you make the most mistakes on. If you want that main book to be perfect, you might want to practice on some smaller, less important stuff first. Nobody does everything right the first time, and trying to do it right will slow you down. My first book took about five years, and I spent months fiddling with the cover design (and it was still terrible). Then I tried to figure out book marketing for a couple years.

The reason most people never make it through their first draft is that they're comparing their rough draft with other people's *finished* books – instead you need to force yourself to get through the book quickly to get the content right. Often the story doesn't emerge until you get through to the end. Then you can start revising and moving things around. After two or three passes, it's *readable.* Then, finally, you can start improving the writing. However, as I said earlier, story matters most for fiction, and content for non-fiction. Fancy, clever writing that you think is really good will probably stand out and distract from the narrative or content. But the point is, don't worry about making the writing beautiful, especially in the early stages, or you'll never finish. And also, maybe put aside that labor of love you've been stuck on for years and try to write something short and simple this month and put it out there.

The key to profitable publishing is learning how to quickly produce books that people want to buy, so it's best to test the market out with some smaller books, even the first few chapters, the premise or main idea of a book, to see what kind of traction it gets.

★ **A note on non-fiction.** I recently talked about publishing on a cruise ship full of entrepreneurs, and explained the difference between a "brand" book and a "benefits" book.

A brand book is the one most entrepreneurs want to write, that defines what they do and why, their mission statement, their reason for being and philosophy of life. Those books are good for positioning and to establish credibility, but not very easy to sell without a platform (because nobody is looking for you, or your company, or your brand yet – especially if you've made up some new words or a catch phrase). It's a lot easier to build a business around a benefits book, that focuses on providing value and helping a very specific group of people solve a very specific problem. Personally, I put out a bunch of benefits books first on cover design, publishing and book marketing – they bring me lots of traffic and qualified leads, so my business grew quickly. Probably this year I'll put out my first major brand book, *Paid to Create*, which will be more interesting now because I can talk about how I built my profitable businesses. Also, a brand book by itself won't generate much income, you still need a product or service that people want and a great offer; and even then, a benefits book will usually be more visible because it has more keywords people are searching for.

The money in publishing is usually in having lots of individual books on specific subjects rather than one big one; but also in having a funnel with backend services. I was using my books to bring me clients; now I use them to get people to join my list or Facebook groups, build trust by providing value, and then offer them an online course or service if they need more support and feedback.

TEST IT OUT WITH BETAREADERS

Finally, it's a good idea to test out your concept with beta readers pretty early in the process. Maybe even after the first few chapters. If you can't share the premise, introduction or first couple chapters and get people to sign up to read more, that could be a problem. And that's something you can test out pretty quickly, before you spend another six months writing. (Create a landing page with a nice book cover, description and sample chapter, say you're looking for beta readers and ask if anyone wants to get early access to the full book for free.)

It's also a good idea to get some feedback from betareaders before you hit publish. I generally give out 100 to 1000 ARCs (advanced review copies) to my betareaders before I launch a book so that they can post reviews quickly once the book is live. I'll talk more about that, and how to build a huge list of potential readers before you publish, a little later.

CHALLENGE #1

This section was about writing the kind of book that sells; however if you're already written your book, you can at least *position it* as the kind of book that will sell – as long as you figure out the popular keywords and categories that readers are actively searching for, what kind of book cover attracts them, and what features or benefits they hope to find. You can then edit your book's subtitle or tagline a bit to include these keywords or elements. Even if your book doesn't exactly fit those categories or keywords, it's usually better to tap into a popular genre or topic rather than label yourself more uniquely with terms nobody is looking for. Before you continue with this book, I want you to *take action.* Spend twenty minutes researching, and share your results in the Guerrilla Publishing Facebook group for feedback.

1. Find your categories and keywords

First, go to Amazon and search for any keywords you think relate to your book. See what comes up. Click on some of those books and find ones that are similar to yours, and are also selling well (generally, look for books with a sales rank lower than #5000.)

Also check out their categories. Make a list of categories that might be a good fit for your book. Ideally, categories where the #1 book's rank isn't crazy low. You want to have a chance to get that #1 slot later, so look for categories where the #1 book is ranked at #1000 or higher (if you can find a less competitive category with the #1 book at a much higher rank, it'll be easier for you to get that orange bestseller sticker).

Try to find categories where the #20 book isn't doing well, maybe over #50,000 – that'll make it easier for your book to at least stick on the first page of that category with less effort.

You can also use keyword tools to see what people are typing into Amazon or Google. I use KindleSpy and KDRocket (from Dave Chesson of Kindlepreneur) but there are free tools you can use as well. We'll revisit keywords later so don't worry too much about it, just start thinking in terms of aligning your book with the terms your readers are using.

2. Make a list of competing titles

Look for 10 or 20 titles that are performing well on Amazon and are similar to your book. Take note of their

23

cover design and description. Try to figure out why they're doing well (this won't always be obvious; it could be that they're spending a lot on ads). But generally, try to see what they have in common. Also try to figure out if they're traditionally published or self-published (trad published books will often have nicer covers but higher prices; indie published books can perform much better even with amateur covers because they are priced lower and the authors are generally more savvy with online marketing).

You want to find your peers – so traditionally published authors who have a readership you covet, and indie published authors who may be interested in teaming up or doing some cross-promotion. This list will be important later so spend some time on it. Find at least five pretty major bestsellers, and at least five indie published books that are selling really well. Also – you might want to do this every week for a few weeks, to see which books are *actually* sticking, as opposed to a flash in the pan book promotion which reaches the top of Amazon, but then sinks again.

3. Craft your author bio

Now that you know the keywords readers are searching for, the bestselling books in your genre, and the categories your book will fit into, try to organize all of that into a short author bio. If you use Amazon Central to claim your book and set up an author account, your author bio will show up on your Amazon page, which is *another place* to add important keywords.

Your author bio will generally say what you write and for whom; which genres you love and why; and your favorite authors. You could also say people have described your writing as "Stephen King meets Dan Brown" but that will probably sound unconvincing. You'll get the same benefits and sound more sincere if you say, "I aim to give readers the same thrills I got from reading Stephen King and Dan Brown."

You'll use some keywords and author names in your book summary later too, but for right now, try to make a one paragraph author bio that lists some famous books, famous authors, a couple quirky facts about you that will endear you to readers (mention things you know your readers also love), and possibly where you live. Cut out everything personal that won't resonate with readers. Add in more specific keywords and details.

4. Craft an elevator pitch

You need to be able to pitch your book in one or two sentences. If you have trouble describing your book, or knowing how to talk about it without launching into a thirty-minute sermon, you're going to have a huge problem getting people to listen. Use your keywords, categories and the books and authors you've collected and try to boil your book summary down into its basic components. Try to use *different* keywords than you used in the author bio, so you don't repeat too much.

I generally put this at the bottom of my Amazon description, to make it more clear for readers and also hit some keywords. For example, my pitch for *Scarlet Thread* is, "Fans of Fallen and Percy Jackson will love this mashup of fallen angels and forgotten gods."

This isn't a great *summary*, because it's descriptive rather than active, and doesn't suck the reader in, but it is a decent pitch – in that it gives readers a pretty clear idea of what it's about and whether or not they'll like it in a very short sentence. It's *fine* to compare your book to famous books or authors, but you do need to be careful. The higher you raise expectations, the more critical readers will be. However it's generally more important to get the conversion and let the reader start reading, then underselling with a more modest description and losing the reader.

INTRODUCE YOURSELF IN THE GUERRILLA PUBLISHING FACEBOOK GROUP

When you think it's pretty good, introduce yourself in the Facebook group with your new bio and blurb. Keep it short and sweet: make sure the genre is clear and that we can get the main idea. You aren't *selling* the book, so don't worry about a hook, you're just trying to introduce yourself and your book in a simple, clear way that will connect with other writers in your genre. You don't need a long summary of what the book is about, or what happens (the plot) – keep your blurb to one or two sentences.

Join the Guerrilla Publishing Facebook group!

2: PUBLISHING

Now that you have an idea of what you're publishing and for whom, we can start to turn your manuscript into the kind of product they want to buy. Publishing isn't really a mysterious or complicated process. It's about turning your book into a professional looking product that attracts readers of your genre, positioning it in a desirable way, and putting it in front of them at a price point they will find reasonable. At the basic level, all you need to do is format your manuscript for print and ebook, and make book covers – then distribute the book to online marketplaces where readers routinely buy their books. The difficult part of this is that, if you have total control over the design process – which you usually will if you're hiring a designer (you're the boss) and you also have never designed a book before, you're going to make decisions based on personal preference rather than market experience. In other words, you'll choose what *you* like instead of what *readers* like and expect. And that will often destroy your book's chances of success.

The wrong cover will make all of your marketing efforts and advertising fail. You'll need to spend ten times as much money and energy trying to get readers to take a chance on your book than you would have if you'd have gotten the cover right. So don't think your book cover is just a small piece of your publishing process, and don't assume that since it's your book, you should get the cover you think best fits the story.

HOW TO MAKE BOOK COVERS THAT SELL

I've probably written half a million words on cover design, but I'll try to condense it all into a few main points that I've found myself repeating over the years.

First, the cover's job is to get readers to start reading the description. Not to sell the book. You can't communicate everything on a cover, and you shouldn't try. It also doesn't matter if the cover matches your book exactly – it only matters that the cover attracts the right readers of your genre enough to get them to read the description.

For fiction, this is mostly about colors and contrast, and a humanizing element. You want to make them feel something. You want it to be beautiful. If you mess it up with too much crap (lots of characters, setting, objects, details) you'll be hitting *conceptual* or cerebral features, not emotional buttons. That's not what you want, because the cover isn't the place to list the benefits or selling points of the book – that's what the description is for. The cover just needs to *attract*, it doesn't need to *sell*.

For non-fiction, the cover should focus on benefits, so the title should often be simple and clever but not enigmatic. It shouldn't be something you need to think about to get. But a good juxtaposition of words can work.

Generally however, the keywords in the subtitle and the promised features and benefits is what will sell non-fiction, so keep it clean and simple. (And test your subtitle! I posted some variations on Facebook to get feedback, then used the best suggestions in my sales copy).

WHY MOST AUTHORS GET THEIR COVERS ALL WRONG

Most authors try to communicate the essence of their book on the cover, and end up with something overwhelming or complex that loses the immediate, emotional impact of something cleaner. It's almost always better to get a pretty premade cover that *could* represent the book than one that you think fits perfectly but doesn't attract readers. Remember, readers haven't read the story yet, so they won't know if the cover doesn't fit everything *exactly*, and they aren't going to mind once they start reading as long as they like the book. In the case of things like a character's eye color or hair color, it's best to get it right if you can, and those are usually simple fixes. But if it's a matter of specific clothing, a particular expression or stance, it will be nearly impossible to find the right stock photos and photoshop everything together convincingly.

Most authors begin their covers with a specific *scene* from the book in mind, which isn't a good idea, not only because it's too complex, but also because you don't want to give the interesting bits of your story away. All you want to do is *hint* at the genre and setting.

Generally, for most fiction, there are three foolproof layouts you can use. One, a flat landscape picture, hopefully at least with a humanizing element (a garment, object, footsteps... something that refers to a character – because without character there is no story). Two, a landscape picture with a character in it; either in the foreground or background. Smaller figures for more epic stories with bigger landscapes; bigger characters for more action and character-driven stories. Three, a face on top and a landscape on the bottom.

These are generally pretty simple, so you can get a cheaper designer to do them reasonably well (the more complex you want your book cover to be, the more you'll need to pay to make it look professional – and even then it's unlikely to sell well because you'll have missed the points I mentioned earlier.

THE ONE MISTAKE THAT WILL
CRIPPLE BOOK SALES

Many authors want to "stand out" and "be different." They hate the idea that all books in a particular genre look the same and they want to offer something new. Which is a really bad idea. Readers expect covers from certain genres to look a certain way. Publishers do that because they're conforming to reader expectations and genre conventions. You want your book to immediately look like it belongs among those other bestselling books you picked out earlier. It should look like it fits in. It can still be *better*, but it shouldn't be *different*.

Things get confusing because if you Google "best book cover designs" you'll find samples of creative literary fiction covers, which are usually strange and imaginative; or remakes of famous books by classic authors which will sell no matter what cover they have. The more creative and unique your cover is, the more work you'll need to do to catch reader's attentions, because they may think it looks cool but won't immediately see that it's the kind of book they enjoy reading.

Be clear before you're clever. When you have a huge audience, and can put a book out and make it a bestseller with no marketing, then you can start taking creative risks with your book covers because your readers will buy it anyway. But in the beginning, let the cover do its job for you and you'll make everything else a thousand times easier.

HIRING A BOOK COVER DESIGNER

There's a lot of competition for book cover designs. For non-fiction, you might be able to get something passable from Fiverr.com. Fiction covers are more complicated. New designers often charge between $200 and $300 for cover design. Some of them are excellent, but once discovered they'll be booked out months in advance, and need to raise their prices. There are also lots of premade cover designers and marketplaces popping up where you can sometimes find a reasonable cover, however often these designers are amateurs and, even if the art is good, the text looks unprofessional. I sometimes find a great piece of art and spend $300 on it, but ask them to remove all the text because I'll need to redo it. So don't assume, if you're paying less than $300, that you're getting a professional design (though you can, absolutely, it's also possible to pay that much and get something terrible).

Also, beginner designers are more likely to bend over backwards trying to make you what they think you want – which can result in a really ugly cover. It's generally better to let designers do their magic, which is why sometimes premade covers look better than something custom they tried to make for a client. In the low-budget range, I don't think you can go wrong with 99designs. You can get lots of different samples from designers, and there are some very talented artists there, for both fiction and non-fiction.

On the higher end, the best cover designers I know charge between $500 and $700, but often have long wait times. I was charging $829 for covers, but I was usually too busy to take on new clients, so I've just raised my price to $1500 and added some bonuses. You can also pay *more* for cover design – I've seen packages up to $2500 for book cover design. In some cases, if you're also getting bonus materials for marketing or promotion, or some expert publishing advice, a higher price might be justified. Higher priced designers may also have time to be more creative and make you something innovative – but like I said earlier, that's usually a risk you don't want to take. Personally I'd start with something from 99designs, which also lets you get some feedback and doing a little premarketing by asking people to help you choose a design. You'll get something that should be more than adequate, and if the book begins earning lots of money, you can spend more on a cover makeover later.

There is a point where a cover is good enough. If it's clean and looks professional, and the genre or subject is pretty obvious, paying more for a different cover might not make any difference. Especially if the book is invisible on Amazon and not getting any traffic. Get something functional, drive some traffic, test your conversion. If you're not selling, it's *probably* not the cover's fault – though if you aren't sure, you can post your cover in my Facebook group and ask for feedback.

However, it's also possible that you have a decent cover that is not clear and obvious – it's not attracting the right readers, or it might be attracting the wrong readers. This will screw up your reviews and also-boughts. If this is the case, you'll probably need an experienced cover designer to figure out what's wrong and how to fix it.

If you want to make your own book cover, it is *possible.* I've actually spent a lot of time trying to make templates and resources for indie authors on a budget who want to DIY their book cover. And I don't like saying only people who can afford a professional cover should be allowed to publish. So if you're broke, do the best you can. I can think of dozens of bestselling authors that started out with terrible book covers. That said, your homemade cover is probably not going to look professional and it will be much harder to convince readers to take a chance on your book. Most of the time, a $20 cover on Fiverr.com will look better than the one you made yourself, and it's usually worth it to save up for a cover instead of spending that money on ads or promotions. Plus, the danger in making your own cover is that you'll waste a ton of time messing around with it, and you'll fall in love with your own creation and be unable to recognize that it's killing sales.

I have a free book on Cover Design Secrets That Sell, you can grab it from my site, www.creativindiecovers.com.

HOW TO FORMAT YOUR BOOK FOR EBOOK

If you've formatted your book well in Word, conversion to ebooks is a snap. I actually have a free online ebook conversion tool you can use, based on Calibre (a free ebook software), at www.Publishxpress.com.

You need to have used paragraph styles, and set the margins and spacings correctly, and used H1 tags on chapter headings so they show up in the navigation pane (all of that is explained in my tutorials on diybookformats. com) but if you've done it right, in a few minutes you'll have a decent mobi and epub file ready to go. You can also just upload the Word file to KDP or Smashwords or Draft2Digital, with varying degrees of success. Conversion like this won't usually handle images well, and it won't embed fonts, but for simple books it'll be good enough.

Ebooks need to be readable and functional, so it's always better to give up some style to make sure that they work across multiple platforms and devices. If you do want to include images, just make sure the originals are at least 1200px or so wide, so they'll fill the screen without getting shrunk on 600dpi surfaces and look tiny. But if you have lots of images, you'll need to pay a delivery fee that will eat into costs (on Amazon at least), so be frugal.

If you want more control and more style, you'll probably need a professional ebook formatter who knows some code. I usually use Sigil, another free book software, to open up my epub file, embed fonts and make sure everything looks OK, before saving and converting into mobi (I just drag my epub file into Kindle Previewer for desktop and it will save a new mobi file – it's not ideal, but it's simple and it works). A professional formatter will usually start from scratch, convert your manuscript to clean html, and code things by hand, but in my experience that's not really necessary.

If you don't want to learn how to do all of this yourself, just find someone to do it for you. I avoided ebook formatting for almost a year before I finally forced myself to overcome the learning curve by taking some courses and getting my hands dirty.

HOW TO FORMAT YOUR BOOK FOR PRINT

Formatting, on the other hand, is probably something you can do yourself. It can be a pain, especially in Microsoft Word, but it's something you can learn how to do if you wrestle with it for a few days, and probably a skillset that will come in handy if you're going to be publishing a lot of books.

There are a few online services or templates that promise a 1-click, simple process for making print books. I wouldn't recommend these. They're too generic and unlikely to look professional. Scrivener also isn't great for making print books, though it may simplify writing and ebook formatting.

At the same time, however, book formatting is pretty standardized. Most fiction and non-fiction books have only a handful of variations.

- Page numbers at the top, or bottom
- Headers and footers centered or outside-aligned
- First paragraph and chapter heading styles

Generally, the more adult the book, the less fancy fonts and styles it will have (bigger design is for younger readers). But you do generally want the chapter title fonts to match the book cover font. And the first paragraph will usually be non-indented and have a little flair (all caps, a different font, bolded first few words). You don't want to do too much though or use conflicting design elements or styles, so keep it simple.

I have dozens of book formatting templates on www.diybookformats.com, along with free tutorial videos. I wrote a whole book about formatting a few years ago but it really is a skill you need to see to learn, so the videos and templates will help you much more than if I tried to describe the process here. I also have a list of my favorite fonts, both free and professional, and some extra bonuses if you sign up for the master package of templates.

Even so, it's not a simple or easy process; it will take some time to learn and it can be frustrating. You can also hire a formatter on Fiverr.com and they may do a reasonable job – just make sure you know whether you're paying to get it formatted in Word or InDesign, and whether they'll send you back the source files so you can make your own changes later.

If you want to hire a more professional formatter, Word formatting usually costs under $100 (but better designers may charge more). InDesign formatting can cost several hundred dollars. Readers may not be able to notice exactly *why* InDesign formatted books look more professional, but it will be a smoother reading experience. The spacing is better and the text will be cleaner. I'll sometimes format quickly in MS Word to put something out there, but after I've made sure I've caught all the typos and the book is fully finished, I'll get it reformatted in InDesign (especially if I'm sending out review copies to reviewers or professional organizations).

What you don't want is to hire someone to do it in InDesign, then discover dozens of typos that didn't get fixed in editing (there are always typos), and then spend weeks going back and forth with the designer to try and weed them all out (this invariably happens every time, which is why I don't offer formatting services anymore). If you need someone to format for you, you can also check out EbookLaunch.com

★ I don't spend much time on my print formatting actually – I could do it a lot better and probably should, because I do sell some print books, but the majority of my sales and downloads are in ebooks.

HOW TO DISTRIBUTE YOUR BOOK

I'm a big fan of Createspace and Kindle Direct Publishing (KDP), but there are limitations to both. In general, Createspace is the easiest platform to use, puts your print on demand books up on Amazon, and also has an expanded distribution option. If you get their free ISBN option, they'll list you in databases bookstores and libraries can access. I go with the free one because it's easier and cheaper than buying your own. The difference is, on the Amazon page for the print book, it may list "Createspace" as the publisher and people can look you up by ISBN and know that you're self-published. For my first few books, I tried to hide that fact by doing everything professionally and using a publishing imprint name and logo. That didn't matter at all. And the truth is, nobody will look up your ISBN. Few readers will care who published your book; plus on the Kindle version you can just set your own publisher name anyway.

The advantage of POD (print on demand) over traditional publishing is that you don't need to order 500 books to get a good deal, store them in your garage for a year, and try to sell them at events or mail them out to buyers one-buy-one. Plus, you want most of your sales to be online so that every sale brings you a boost in sales rank and visibility. Also, selling online is so much cheaper and easier, because you can reach more people with less effort, but we'll talk more about that later.

Among POD services, many indie authors recommend Lightning Source (IngramSpark) over Createspace, because (they argue) the quality is better and it's easier to get into bookstores. Based on those arguments, I went that way with my first few books. Here is what I learned:

1. The quality might be better, but that mainly depends on design and formatting. If you format a book in InDesign it will look slightly better from Lightning Source, and it's true that Createspace sometimes has some quality issues. However, Lighting Source is also much pickier about file specifics. If you aren't a designer, prepare for a lot of headaches trying to get all your files exactly compliant to their standards. Plus, they have a setup fee for uploading files. So each round of making changes + uploading new files can be expensive and take a long time. Since print book sales aren't my main focus anyway, it's not worth it to me to wrestle with Lightning Source. However if you want to do everything professionally, perfectly, and don't expect there to be lots of changes (which is true for almost all authors the first time) you might want to check them out, as long as you have a great designer who is willing to work with you to troubleshoot why the files keep getting rejected.

2. Libraries and bookstores probably won't stock your book. Even if you set your discount at 60%, which is standard, and offer full refunds to bookstores, which will quickly put you into massive debt, they still won't order copies unless they are likely to sell. So first, they might look you up on Amazon to see how many reviews you have or check the sales rank. Libraries may request a copy or two if you get some good press or if someone recommends it, but you don't want to focus on trying to sell a copy at a time. That said, I've had universities and bookstores bulk order my books from Createspace directly.

Trying to do everything perfectly is how most authors waste a lot of time and money the first time around. What I'm encouraging you to do, is learn how to publish quickly and cheaply, so you can focus your time and money on building a solid author platform or setting up marketing funnels that keep your books visible. That said, for business books or if you plan to do a lot of events or use the book to get speaking gigs or build up your reputation, quality does matter, so you may want to hire the best designer you can find and get set up on Lightning Source. This might also be one of the instances when a small press or publishing service can really help, since they'll be able to design and upload all the files and will be used to this process – however you shouldn't sign away a huge cut of your profits just for administrative work like that... unless they can also help sell it, which they probably can't.

HOW TO DISTRIBUTE YOUR EBOOK

For ebooks, you mainly want to focus on Kindle, iBooks and Kobo, but there are several other stores. The easiest way to do it is to use Smashwords, or the newer Draft2Digital (my choice, because it's a little easier to use). Both will distribute your ebook to the larger online stores and take 10%. You can save a little if you publish with iBooks directly, though it can be a hassle if you're not a Mac user. Those sites will generally accept a Word file or an epub file.

However, I prefer to start out in KDP Select, which means you just need the mobi file (you can also upload a

Word file to KDP). Focusing on one platform means you can concentrate your sales in one place and keep your rank up higher. Generally you'll also earn more in KDP Select, but we'll discuss this more later.

What some authors are tempted to do instead, is sell from your own website so you don't have to pay Amazon a bunch of money to sell for you. Almost always, this is a big mistake – because then you'll be trying to sell books one by one, and probably need to handle distribution and fulfillment. It's like standing outside of a bookstore trying to sell books from your trenchcoat. Difficult to do. What you want to do instead is to train Amazon and the internet to sell your book for you, so you can go fishing (or watch TV, or write more books).

The *exception* is if you're selling a very specialized, high priced ebook – in which case you can charge much more if selling from your website, but will need to drive your own traffic. Even in this case, however, I'd put a shorter book or sample on Amazon to boost visibility, and then get them back to your list with a free offer (as an alternative or addition to advertising or other forms of promotion).

HOW TO GET POD HARDBACKS
AT A REASONABLE PRICE

Just kidding... there isn't really a way to get cheap POD hardbacks. If you need hardback covers made, you can get them from Lulu or Lightning Source, but they're both prohibitively expensive. You may want to make some available as a giveaway prize, or to send out to big reviewers, but you're unlikely to make any money with them. Traditional publishers use hardbacks because they don't cost much more to print than paperback, but publishers can charge much more for them. So hardbacks have the highest profit margin – which is usually why they put hardbacks out first and paperbacks a few months later.

But that only works if you're ordering thousands of books at once, something you don't want to do unless you can move them at events (which can be effective, though there are easier ways to move books). Generally I skip hardbacks, since they take more investment and effort and don't impact my sales income.

HOW TO GET FULL COLOR BOOKS MADE

Getting full print color books made is also problematic. You *can* get them printed at Createspace, but it'll be expensive. They charge per page, not per illustration, so even if you only want a handful of color pictures inside the book, you'll have to charge far too much to make a profit, and people still won't buy them. What I'd suggest is making some available, with Createspace or Blurb.com (finer quality but more expensive), and using them as gifts or for reviewers, but mostly relying on the black and white paperback version. It won't look as good, but you'll be able to sell it at a reasonable price. The ebook will show in color depending on the device. And you can have a link or offer in the back to get the full color PDF from your website if they want to see it.

WHO CARES ABOUT GETTING INTO BOOKSTORES?

I think it's every author's dream to be in bookstores and have a great looking book on the shelf. The problem is that most bookstores operate by stocking books to see what sells, and getting refunds from publishers on all the books that don't sell. You can try to get books into specific bookstores on consignment – I've done that before, by targeting small or indie bookstores one by one. I'd send a couple books, they'd sell them, and then I'd get a check for $12 or something. So much work and effort for that much money, for those two books. Now, I sell about 50 ebook copies a day (per book) on Amazon without doing anything, and a few dozen print copies a month.

Bookstores are still important, and I'd like to get some books there later, but it's not easy (or desirable) for most indie authors. In the week it takes of effort to get a bookstore to stock your book, you could have built a complete online platform that does your marketing for you. Plus, bookstores will usually stock books they've heard about that get good press. So if you set up with Createspace's expanded distribution, and get some amazing press (I'll talk about how to do that later), small bookshops who are interested might order a few copies. After my books are doing really well, and I have a profitable funnel, I might want to get a virtual assistant to research a thousand indie bookshops and email them about my book – but generally, if you can't sell your book on Amazon, the biggest marketplace, you're going to have trouble convincing anyone else to take it either.

GETTING MORE VISIBILITY ONLINE

So let's talk more about your Amazon page. This could also be your iBooks page or any other "sales page" where your book is hosted. The two important features of this page are visibility and conversion.

First the page has to be seen. If it isn't seen, nothing else matters. It doesn't matter what your cover looks like, or how much you charge, or what keywords you use. Nobody will read the amazing description you've written. So you need to *boost visibility* to this page.

1. You can use keywords that people are searching for in your description and author bio, and even in your editorial reviews.

2. You can get links pointing directly to your Amazon page using anchored keywords (use the clean link to your Kindle book which ends after the ASIN number. For example, here's a link to my young adult mermaid book.) I put links like that, using relevant keywords, on several of my blogs. If your blog or website is new and doesn't have any domain authority, try guest posting on some bigger blogs (links from authoritative domains carry more weight. You can check out your domain authority with this free online tool). I'll usually also post a PowerPoint on SlideShare, a video on YouTube, and content on a few more sites to get more links pointing back to my blog and/or Amazon page. I'm trying to create a "web" of links around my keywords which all focus on my Amazon page.

All of these pieces of content can get found by people searching for my keywords. I usually also make a post like "top 10 best young adult mermaid books for teens." If you're doing something very competitive, like "best vampire books" it will be hard for your content to show up or rank well. However, even though there are probably a million blog posts, not that many people are putting out videos or PowerPoints or other forms of content on the same topics. I chose "young adult mermaid books" in big part because it's much less competitive, so it's easy for my content to start showing up in Google search results. People find my content, and my links, and end up on my Amazon page.

TESTING YOUR CONVERSIONS

We'll talk more about making your book "sticky" (so it sticks with a high rank in your category) later, and how to use the above tactics in your book launch. But for now let's move on to the other important piece of your Amazon page: *conversion*.

Let's say someone, somehow discovers your book on Amazon. Maybe it showed up in a natural search result, or maybe in somebody's also-boughts, or maybe you've paid to have your book show up in front of them.

If they're the right reader (someone who enjoys your genre or is interested in your topic), and they see the cover and title, and it's attractive or looks like something similar to the other books they enjoy, they'll click the link and view your main Amazon page. If the cover still looks good, they'll scan the description. It should capture their imagination by being a mix of the familiar and the new (elements they are familiar with, but with new and exciting twists). They should get a sense of the story, setting and major conflict. If it's a romance, both major characters should be described, as well as the opposition between them. If the description sounds interesting, they'll check the reviews, and finally the price.

People don't believe five-star reviews, so having a bunch of five-star reviews won't help. They'll usually read the best and the worst; along with all the ones on the first page that have been voted "most helpful." It's best to get about 20 reviews, with a couple twos or threes thrown in, and an average of at least 4 stars.

The price is the last consideration, so having a flash, low price deal won't do much (unless it's on a deals website and they're book hoarders). Generally, 99cents and 2.99 seems to sell about the same, but can cause differences in reader satisfaction (readers might be fine with a shorter 99cent book and enjoy it, but leave negative reviews if the same book is 2.99 because they were expecting more). Test pricing out; generally 2.99 is a safe price, with monthly 99cent promos to keep the rank in the top of its category.

If everything looks good, many of the people who find your Amazon page will buy the book. Then you have a high conversion rate. It's not easy to do. But luckily you can keep improving it. Start with some paid ads – try to get 100 clicks to your Amazon page. It might cost $50 or so. Out of those 100 clicks, people you know were interested in your ad and saw your page, how many of them actually bought the book? I think, generally, a 10% conversion rate is a good start. But that's also a lot of waste – you'll need to get 1000 people to see the book for every 100 sales. Still pretty good, and you can just spend lots on ads to keep selling, but it may be difficult to stay in the black this way. It's *easier* and cheaper to keep working on your conversion rate.

First, if your cover is the problem, you need a new one. One way to test it is, run two Facebook ads, one with the cover art, and one without it. Which one gets more clicks? Try a new cover or different picture or piece of pretty art. Does it get more clicks with the same description? But conversion is low? Then you need a new cover.

If the cover is good enough, and people like it, you're losing them with a lackluster description or lack of reviews (or poor quality reviews).

IS YOUR BOOK SUMMARY GOOD ENOUGH?

I'm not an expert in book description, but I know it's usually difficult to write your own, and that making it better can drastically improve your conversion. My test is to see whether my sales rank holds the same after a promotion. If you get a hundred downloads in a day and get up to the top #1000 books on Amazon, you'll get a lot more visibility. If your book cover is good and your description is great, you should keep converting a lot of those new viewers. But you won't get them all. Rank will drop quickly, but it shouldn't keep dropping *forever*. It should level out, hopefully somewhere above 10,000. If it doesn't, you need to keep improving things until it does. After 10,000, visibility will get worse and rank will keep slipping until you're invisible again.

So tweak, do some promotion, watch your rank, tweak again. Until you can make your book stick or level out, it's not a good idea to spend a lot on promotion or advertising, because most of the traffic you're driving isn't buying the book. Maybe they'd *love* the book, but the cover, description and reviews weren't enough to convince them to buy it. You've lost your one chance to impress that reader with your writing.

Some tips:

- Use keywords, but don't stuff them in or make it unnatural. Also keywords aren't usually a good hook to catch attention, so I'd add them in later, towards the bottom.
- The first sentence should probably be a header or bold, and it has to hook and captivate.
- The first paragraph should get into the story immediately, and not in a generic summary. Get real and personal with your characters and world. Share the conflicts. Show what makes your story or world different (what's your unique selling proposition?)
- Then you can add credibility boosters like keywords, reviews and other things – though sometimes this can seem like you're trying too hard.

I've seen short, one paragraph summaries make bestsellers, but I've also seen overblown, hyperbolic descriptions comparing the book to the Hungers Games and Harry Potter, listing all the Goodreads ratings and having a dozen reviews. I don't think there's a formula because I've seen so many different things work. But if yours isn't working, try another. (It's OK to get *ideas* from other books in your genre, but make sure you change everything so it's not just a clone or copy).

You can **edit and style** your description in KDP or Createspace, but you have to use html (code) for formatting. Also KDP and Createspace have recently started to integrate more, so that you can publish both ebook and print book on the same platform, but it's not a smooth process. However, you can also set up an account with author central and claim the book there – then edit the description with a more standard text editor that allows more style choices (bold, italic, etc). You want to avoid having one big block of text.

WHY YOUR REVIEWS ARE BEING DELETED

Reviews are really important to help with conversion. People won't trust all raving 5-star reviews, so don't worry if you get a few negative ones – they'll just add credibility to the positive ones. We'll talk about how to get reviews later, but for now, you need to understand Amazon's review policy. They want natural, unbiased reviews from people who have no relationship with the author. This obviously makes it difficult for authors to ask their fans to write reviews; Amazon may delete those reviews as well as any from friends or family. Reviews go missing all the time, which can be annoying after you've worked so hard to get them. But Amazon's first priority is to make buyers feel comfortable so they keep shopping.

Some things you can do to protect your reviews:

1. When you link to your book, use the direct link ending in the ASIN number (the remaining part of the URL has tracking information; if you're logged in, Amazon will know who sent them).
2. Don't email the link directly in your email or on your Facebook wall: write a blog post with the link, and send them to that.

It used to be the policy that readers who got an ARC copy *had* to say "I got this book for free in exchange for a review." But Amazon started deleting *those* reviews, or anything that said "in exchange for" or something similar – because they don't want you paying for reviews, even with free books or merchandise. I send out advanced copies of my books to reviewers, but not *in exchange* for reviews. I just give them books, and hope that they will review, but I don't make it mandatory (so when they post reviews on Amazon, they don't have to use the "in exchange" phrase).

While you want to know about this stuff and be careful, you also shouldn't stress about it too much. Focus on reaching new readers, getting them on your list, and encouraging them to review will be easier and faster than contacting Amazon and trying to get them to restore your reviews.

HOW TO REMOVE NEGATIVE REVIEWS FROM YOUR BOOK

One last thing you should know about reviews: readers can vote reviews as helpful or unhelpful. The most helpful reviews show up on the first page of Amazon. However, I believe that negative reviews are more likely to be voted on, and also that many of these votes come from readers who haven't read the book. Readers skim the positive reviews, and if they look good, they'll buy. They don't go back and vote for positive reviews later, even if they liked it. Readers also skim the negative reviews, and if they agree with whatever the reviewer didn't like *in general,* they won't buy the book – and they'll vote that review "helpful" because they agree with it. So what tends to happen, on most books, is that the bad reviews rise to the top.

If you build a list of fans, you can ask them for a favor; to go to Amazon and vote on some of the positive reviews as helpful, so they show up on your first page to displace the negative ones. Be careful asking your fans to do things like this though, as it can sometimes backfire – but only in the case that you have an irate reviewer angry over a sensitive topic, who thinks you're using your hoard of fans to manipulate Amazon. Many books have an overwhelming majority of positive reviews, and only a few bad ones, so having those negative reviews show up first is actually misleading to new readers, who will read those outliers rather than all the positive reviews that are more common. You can't really delete negative reviews, but you can at least alter the presentation so that those aren't the first thing people see. You're only manipulating readers if those negative reviews are totally true, and all the positive ones are fake, and you're trying to trick readers into buying your book anyway... which I would never suggest.

Positive and negative reviews begin with setting reader expectation. I actually try to keep expectations low, by avoiding hyperbole or lots of raving description or reviews. Readers go into it with lower expectations, and are pleasantly surprised and review me well. That's one of the reasons why, for example, I don't tell people I have a Ph.D. or that I'm a bestselling author (usually... though I decided to try it on the cover for this book). They might expect more, and be more critical in their reviews. So if you *manipulate* or mislead readers, you'll suffer for it with harsh reviews. But that doesn't mean you shouldn't pay attention to which reviews show up first on your Amazon page. They're a big part of your conversion. Personally, I don't watch my reviews closely, and if the negative reviews that show up first are fair, I leave them. But sometimes you'll get a review that hits a nerve, and will turn lots of people away from your book, even if it's not true – and you shouldn't let that impact sales.

One time a reviewer accused me of plagiarism, because I'd pulled two sentences from Wikipedia and a passage from an old book of mythology (I was legally in the clear on both, and they were important to the story, though she's right I should have paraphrased them better so they weren't identical). But this one star review was scathing and personal. If it had shown up on the first page, it would have damaged sales. But, if I had gotten fans to downvote it, she could have driven a campaign against me and gotten more people to upvote it. These things happen. I mostly ignored it.

I did leave a comment on her review on Amazon though. Normally, you never want to reply to negative reviews or try to explain yourself, because it rarely ends well. Almost everyone will tell you *never* to respond to a negative review. In this case however, that review is still on Amazon, and if people read it without any context or defense from me, they might believe it. So I left a comment thanking her, and saying I'd removed the problematic passages.

KEYWORDS AND CATEGORIES

In step one, we did research to find the keywords readers are using to find your book, and you used some of those in your description and Amazon bio. But when you upload your files to Createspace or KDP, they'll ask you to choose some categories and keywords. It's confusing, however, because they don't actually show you all the categories you can get into. For many categories, you need to use specific keyword phrases in the keyword box to show up. You can check out the categories on this list here and find some you want to be in; then use those keywords to get in (in the keywords box, enter the ones to unlock the categories, not the ones you think people will be searching for).

You want to pick categories that aren't so competitive, so you can stay high in the charts. However, you can actually get added to *up to 10 categories* by contacting customer support and requesting them. That means, if you aren't exactly sure which category is best, it's fine because you can pick many. The three categories you're ranking highest in will display up on top (as long as you're ranking well, in the top 100 I think). The other categories will show up down below. I choose categories where my resting rank (the average sales rank when I'm not promoting) is enough to get #1 – which means my book displays the orange bestseller sticker – which boosts conversions. The resting rank for my book *Scarlet Thread* right now is about #2500, but I have a friend who also has the orange bestseller sticker and her rank is about #8500 – because she's listed in several less competitive categories. So be on the lookout for categories where the #1 book actually isn't ranking that well, and see if you can beat it.

AUDIO BOOKS

Audiobooks can be worth making, if your books are selling. From what I've heard, you can expect audiobook sales to be 10% to 25% of your normal book sales. So if you sell $1000 in books a month, you might make $250 a month in audiobook sales.

However, producing audiobooks can be expensive, you pay (at the lower end) $100 to $200 per finished hour of narration. One finished hour is equal to about 10,000 words. So for the 70K novel I'm producing right now, I've offered $100 per finished hour and will pay $700 total if the narrator accepts (which they might not... they may counter with a higher rate).

But assuming I get it for $700, it will take a while to earn that money back. At 99cents my book stays in the 2500 range, at $2.99 it stays in the 5000 range. With page reads, I seem to earn more at 99cents, so I'll stay there for now... I think I might make $1000 this month on that one book, but that seems rare – it'll probably drop considerably. Let's say I normally earn $400 per month for that book. 25% is $100 – so it would take me 7 months to pay off the money I spent producing the audiobook.

The problem is, most books aren't making anywhere near that much money. If you can't get your book to sell, you won't earn from your audiobooks or print books (which are usually more like 10% of ebook sales). So getting audiobooks produced at first is probably a mistake, unless you already have a big platform or big marketing budget.

INTERNATIONAL RIGHTS

Some authors, whose books aren't selling, start thinking about translation or international publishing rights. This is also something I would advise against. If you can't make your book sell in the biggest, English language Amazon stores, you're not going to have much luck selling the rights either. *If* you sell a lot of books in the Amazon store, agents, publishers and rights managers might approach you. Or at least you could negotiate a pretty good offer.

That said, I sold the rights to my first book to Russia's biggest publisher and got a nice check from it. They reached out to me because of all the promotion, marketing and publicity I was getting in magazines and major websites. (These days, I wouldn't do all of that publicity, because I don't think it actually sells that many books... but it was good to get visibility from foreign publishers in this case).

There are also new platforms popping up that make it easier for translators or foreign publishers to find and translate your books, though you need to be careful and read the terms and details. I expect this to be a bigger trend over the next few years.

AFFILIATE LINKS

Something else you could be doing, is signing up for Amazon associates and getting affiliate links for your own books – so when you recommend your book and someone goes to Amazon to look for it, you'd get an extra bonus for them using your link. *But more than that,* you can earn a commission on *anything* they buy on Amazon, within a certain number of hours from having clicked your link. There are even tools to extend that period to up to 24 hours (I'm not going to recommend them here because they seem a bit dodgy... but if you can drive people to Amazon using your links near major shopping days, that could be a big win for you).

CHALLENGE #2

1. Set up your Amazon page.
2. Run some Facebook ads.
3. Ask for feedback in the G.P. Facebook group.

It's OK if your ads aren't profitable right now. Just spend $5 boosting a post about your book to your ideal audience. You want to see if A) you can get anyone to click B) whether people who click buy or preorder the book.

3: LAUNCHING YOUR BOOK

Finally, we get to the good stuff. The first two sections might have been basic for some authors, especially if you're only here for "Guerrilla Marketing Hacks." I hope this section will satisfy you.

Firstly, some terminology. *Book Marketing* is generally about telling other people about your book, through advertising or promotion. It doesn't work very well, which is why I wrote *Book Marketing is Dead* a few years ago.

When I ask my audience what their biggest frustrations are, they usually say things like, they don't have time to do any marketing because they should be writing. One author was specifically looking for "The most time-efficient way to manage an ongoing, never-ending marketing strategy." That sentence represents everything I think is wrong with traditional book marketing. The idea that you constantly need to promote or share your book to find new readers is a myth. If you need to *constantly* market your book, you haven't set up an author platform or a marketing funnel that attracts readers and turns them into buyers, which is what I've tried to do my first year. My first course, *Reach Your Readers*, was all about that stuff. My next course, the *21*

Day Bestselling Author Platform, will cover a lot of the same topics, but will focus on setting up an author platform more quickly, focusing on just one task a day for three weeks.

However, *this book* isn't about setting up an author platform. It's about launching a book quickly, in three days or less, without a platform, and getting it to continue selling long-term without more marketing or promotion. Obviously, it's best to do both, but that may not be an option for everyone. My main point is that marketing shouldn't be *ongoing*. Instead, spend a month building a strong author platform, launch really well and make your book a bestseller, then go back to writing more books. Do some promotion and a launch campaign every time you bring out a new book, but don't worry about promoting and marketing *all the time.*

Also, I should warn you that most of the tips in the rest of this book aren't free. I see a lot of authors asking for the best *free* methods to promote books online, and there aren't many. The best way to do it is to build a powerful author platform that gets lots of traffic, but that takes a lot of work and a lot of time. But if you don't have any money, and you have a lot of time, that's what you should do. That's what I did my first year publishing fiction, and I'll continue building great content that attracts natural traffic.

Now, however, when I'm getting ready to publish a new book, I don't do much marketing at all. But I do spend some money. I'm OK spending money because I can accurately project what kind of earnings I'll see. Even so, marketing and advertising can be a risk sometimes, if you don't sell as much as you hope to. The nice thing about advertising, however, is you can start *very cheaply*, for about $5 a day, and test results, *until your ads are profitable.* Then you can simply scale up and spend much more.

In this section I'm going to mention most of the fast, easy and amazingly effective book launch strategies I've learned over the past year. Keep in mind I'm not making tons of money yet, though I am making far more than the average author already, in my first year of writing fiction. So my experience is likely to have knowledge gaps – there are probably things I'm missing. I will be testing all of these out soon though, with fiction and non-fiction book launches, that I'm going to turn into case studies to put inside the Guerrilla Publishing companion course.

★ Typical publishing contracts for first time authors is less than $10,000, and most don't earn out the advance. Most self-publishing authors need to spend around $5,000 to launch their first book, but I publish for free because I've learned how to do everything myself. But because I'm self-publishing, I can not only publish much faster, but I'll also earn more money with every launch, because I'm actively building my platform.

CROWDFUNDING

I've seen some authors try to kickstart their career by running a crowdfunding campaign for a book. This is usually a mistake. It *can* get you some visibility, but usually the amount needed to publish is considerably overpriced. If you're trying to crowdfund $5000, you need to presell thousands of copies. That's really hard to do, even if you have a large platform, but nearly impossible if you don't. And setting up a crowdfunding campaign that doesn't get funded can be a little embarrassing. I'll admit, I did one for my first book (rookie mistake) and it was successful. Might have gotten me some extra visibility. But it was a lot of work: when you do that kind of project, you also need to handle fulfillment, which means production and distribution – I had to mail out all the rewards I'd promised and it was a huge chore: with the shipping costs, I lost money.

If you *do* have a huge platform, producing a book this way can make a lot of sense. John Lee Dumas used Kickstarter to launch his *Freedom Journal* this way and raised $453,803. I've seen Jeff Goins and Jonathan Fields do something similar, by preselling book packages to their followers (buy 10 books and get into a private mastermind group, or other bonuses for bulk orders). We'll talk more about those later. But generally, ideas like that won't work very well until after you've built a platform and following. You're *first point of contact* with a potential reader should not be asking them for money; it should be establishing value.

TO PRESELL OR NOT TO PRESELL

One of the first major questions you'll face is whether to put your book up for preorder. The advantage of putting books up on preorder is that you have a longer launch window – you can put your book up months before the publication date, which gives your book a chance to show up and be seen while people are searching for things, before you've even finished the book. Also, on most platforms, those preorder sales will kick in when you launch, boosting your sales rank for extra visibility. Most indie authors who make a run at the USA Today or NYT Bestseller lists focus on driving sales to their preorder books, then also do a big launch, for maximum sales (most bestseller lists require you to go wide, and publish on iBooks, Kobo and other sites in addition to Amazon).

With Amazon however, preorder sales don't boost rank on launch day. Actually, I think Amazon "freezes" your sales rank a little when you launch after a preorder, which can be frustrating if you're running ads and not seeing the big spike you were hoping for. The preorder sales boost your rank as they come in, but they try to keep things steady and for about 48 hours after you launch, your rank may not reflect sales.

That threw me at first, but I still use preorders for my books because,

- I like being able to share and start marketing books months before they launch.
- Putting a book up on preorder motivates me to get it done in time to launch.*
- There's more time to build up my also-boughts section and test my keywords and categories before I really start marketing.
- You can get reviews posted before you launch your book.*

★ If you *don't* upload a final version of your book in time, Amazon will block you from using preorders for a full year.

I did that a couple years ago. Also, if your finished file isn't uploaded in time, readers may actually get your unedited rough draft with embarrassing notes to yourself (I did that this time. It sucks, but I apologized to my list and sent them a link to the correct file). If you're a procrastinator like me, preorders can be dangerous and risky, but they also push me to get things *done.*

★ When your book is on preorder, people can't review the ebook. But you can set up the print version, make it available on Amazon, then upload a new file and *not approve it.* The print book will show as unavailable, but will still be there (because it *was* published). Then you can send out ARC copies of your book to readers, and send them to the print book on Amazon to review it – the print and ebook versions are on the same Amazon page so those reviews will show up.

GO WIDE OR KDP SELECT?

This is the next big decision you need to make. Some authors don't like giving Amazon so much control, and don't feel comfortable signing a three month exclusivity contract to get into KDP Select. If you're in KDP Select, readers who pay the monthly fee for Kindle Unlimited can read your book for free, and you get paid for page reads.

The alternative is to "go wide" – which means publishing your ebook on multiple platforms. The idea is, you want to make your book available in the formats readers prefer, rather than forcing them to use Amazon, and you want more visibility (as Mark Coker of Smashwords puts it, you don't want to be in just one bookstore, you want to be in *all* bookstores.)

However, online bookstores don't work like normal bookstores. If you get a sale, your sales rank will go up, leading to more visibility. I recommend starting on KDP Select, because if it's your first book and you don't have a big platform, you're going to need to work for every single sale. Let's say you get 1 sale a day, or 30 a month. If you spread those out on 5 platforms, your rank won't see much of a boost, and you'll still be pretty much invisible. But 30 sales on *one* platform (Amazon) *might* be enough for you to get some extra visibility, which could lead to 5 or 10 more sales... which could snowball upwards until you're selling a lot of books. Plus it's easier to focus on just one platform rather than trying to manage several.

Also, it takes time to build up your sales page and book conversion – the more books you sell, the more Amazon or other platforms are going to start recommending you. They *want* to help you sell books, but you need to show them that certain readers are willing to buy your book. As Chris Fox says in *Six Figure Author*, you need to train Amazon to sell for you.

I know some people that do well going wide, but it usually takes six months or more, and they are usually driving quite a bit of their own traffic. I think once you're already established and have a readership or email list hungry for your books, you can try going wide and probably make it work. That said, I also have friends who sell loads of books, who tried going wide, saw their income plummet, and quickly returned to KDP Select. That's because, in

KDP Select, it's not just about the sales: sales get you more visibility, which can result in more borrows and page reads, which can easily double your income.

I did use Smashwords a few years ago, and have been using Draft2Digital to put out permafree books to build my platform (I write young adult, and found that the majority of younger YA readers are on iBooks and downloading free stories... so I found a lot of fans that way). But when I want a book to earn money, I keep books in KDP Select. Some of the strategies that follow will be focused on Amazon, but I'll include promotional tips for marketing books that are wide as well.

It's a complex decision, but basically, if you can do well in KDP Select, you won't need to go anywhere else; and if you can't do well in KDP Select, you probably won't succeed on other platforms either. There are exceptions, of course... if you write a certain genre for a certain demographic and those people are more likely to be reading Nooks for some reason... but it's easier to reach more people, for less money, on Amazon than on other platforms.

★ Mark Coker warns against the power of Amazon in the coming years... and he's right: putting all your eggs in one basket can be risky. Amazon could change its policies at any time. Personally, I want my books to earn as much as possible right now. I can move my books later if the gravy train dries up.

★ Amazon just introduced a new "Prime" readership option. My friend Michelle Madow got an unexplained boost after a free campaign, and after a year of hard work, is suddenly at the top of Amazon. There's no *obvious* reason for this massive boost in rank, but it seems to be due to Prime – a program that for now is only available to authors in KDP Select.

ARE BOOK AWARD CONTESTS WORTH IT?

I signed up for (and won) some book award contests with my first books, but I don't do them anymore. Book awards can be good for some visibility and validation. And it's nice to call yourself an "award-winning author." If you're starting with no platform and have the money, go for it. That said, I don't think many readers of your genre are on those book award sites, and most readers for most genres don't really pay attention to awards (some do, and awards are more important for some genres).

Basically, book awards could be one of the final motivators for an unconvinced reader to take a chance on your book. If they're unconvinced, that's probably because your cover, blurb or reviews aren't strong enough. Fix those and you won't need any book awards. Also, there's the reader expectation factor: awards may raise expectations leading to more critical reviews.

Some enormous, reputable book awards would be amazing to win; and winners of those awards will get lots of press and media. Those awards are often not really accessible to indie authors, and the book awards that are aimed at supporting indie authors don't have the same kind of credibility or visibility boost.

DO YOU REALLY NEED A BLOG
OR AUTHOR WEBSITE?

The short answer: *no*. The reason I like having a blog or website, is that I can put content there that gets traffic, build some backlinks, and it will bring in new readers forever with no effort. Plus the traffic will grow with every launch or promotion.

I started publishing fiction in 2016 and built www. urbanepics.com. I haven't done much with it, or focused on building traffic, but it gets an average of 300 visitors a day in natural search results. That's about 10,000 people a month that might also want to check out my books. If you have time but no money, you should be blogging. My course *Reach Your Readers* has lots of information about what kind of content to develop, but basically, you want to write about things people are searching for; you want to feature other books and authors in your genre, and you want to create massive-value posts ("value bombs") that get shared.

Here's a screenshot of some of the search terms people are finding me for. It's a lot of stuff about mermaids, because my first book was a mermaid romance and I wrote some articles about mermaids to get this kind of traffic. I *should* be doing that for every book and every subject. The trick is to find interesting topics that haven't been covered a million times by other bloggers; or to do specific, wrap-up posts.

Search Engine Terms	▲
Today Yesterday	<u>Summaries</u>
Search	Views
where do mermaids sleep	2
how do mermaids mate	1
mermaids making out	1
what do mermaids do to humans	1
mermad matting	1
book based on mythology	1
how do mermaids have sex?	1
show real pictures of mermaids having sex	1
book where girl becomes mermaid bird creature	1
Other search terms	2
Unknown search terms	57
Total search terms	69

For example, an easy one I recommend, is writing a "top 10 best new (genre) books of (Month, Year)."

- Top ten amazing new scifi books with aliens, March 2017
- Best new paranormal romance books with angels, 2017

It's true that dating this may backfire in the future, but you could remove the dates. The advantage to doing it monthly, is that you always have new content, and you can email that content out to your growing email list every month. You can *also* use your affiliate links, to make some money by promoting other people's books. You can get a virtual assistant to research these for you. The bonus advantage is that the authors you feature will probably share your article, if you tag them on Twitter or message them privately on Facebook and share the link with them (assuming your author website looks clean and professional, which is important).

Sometimes it's hard, though, to grow a single-author blog or have enough content. It's a lot *faster* to build a multi-author blog, which is why I also set up www.theyashelf.com. Interestingly, that site isn't getting as much traffic, probably because I haven't been focused on driving traffic to it or building it up (I'll start doing that this year).

Having a blog and putting the right content on it brings in natural traffic, which will make things a lot easier and cut down on your marketing budget. Plus, it gives you your own real estate, so you aren't just building on someone else's property. This week, one of my Facebook groups, which had over 1200 members, suddenly vanished for no reason. We got it restored a week later but if we hadn't, we would have lost a lot of valuable content. That's one of the reasons you should think about controlling your own space.

Yes, I think you should have a blog or website. No, I don't think you need to blog all the time, or write articles if you're just spinning your wheels or don't know what to write about, or aren't getting any traffic anyway. You need to spend a few weeks building the right kind of content (or hiring it out) and doing some basic set up so the blog can grow. Generally you also need a website so you can be building an email list, however there are ways around it: you can send people straight to an optin box or form (you can make those with most email service providers... for example, this link goes straight to my optin offer for this book, it's just a Mailchimp form). You could also just make a landing page for your book, with no articles or content. More of a static website rather than a blog. A great landing page will convert will, so it's ideal for a free offer or sales page... but then you have to drive all the traffic with paid ads or guest posts, and generally it's hard to make any money if you're selling cheap ebooks. But you could do that if you're selling a high-priced PDF on your own website.

In my case, this book for example will be part of a funnel leading to more products, services and the companion course. So I could set up a landing page and spend money driving people towards it, to get them to sign up, go through my free challenge or video series, and hopefully buy the course if they need more support or are ready for some advanced book marketing tactics. But I could probably get the same amount of visibility and optins, with much less effort, simply by making the book permafree on Amazon and directing people to it from my websites. I might test both.

BONUS TIP: the other thing I use my blogs and websites for is to boost my Amazon SEO. I'll add a lot of keyword anchor links pointing straight to my book on Amazon, like every time I casually mention my <u>young adult mermaid novel</u>. I have a lot of sites, and they have great site authority, which means the links are powerful, and because "mermaid" isn't a very competitive keyword anyway, my book shows up in the first page of search results on Amazon when people search for that term. That's partly because I've done my book description well, but also, I think, because of all the links on the internet pointing to my book using my keywords.

When I hear people ask whether they *need* a blog or website, it's probably because their blog or website isn't well designed, they don't know what to put on it anyway, and it isn't selling any books or getting any optins. So yeah, if your blog is doing *nothing* for you, don't waste time on it. However, if you learn to do it right, blogging doesn't have to be a full time, exhausting strategy. It's something you set up once and then write maybe a post or two a month. This book isn't about setting up an author platform though. So let's skip to the fun stuff.

HOW TO BUILD A HUGE LIST BEFORE YOU LAUNCH

Before I published my first book, I built a new email list of over 8500 young adult readers who were interested in my genre. Since then it's grown to over 25K.

Some people may question the efficacy of lists to sell books, especially since I built my list using free books and giveaways. They may claim I'm "training readers" not to pay for books or to expect free stuff. They may point out that a 25K list probably has horrible open and click through rates.

Here's my response: I don't primarily use my list to sell books. I use them for reviews and visibility. It's true I don't get great engagement from the list I built using giveaways and free books. It has a 20.5% open rate and a 4.8% click rate. Which means I can generally get about 1000 clicks on something when I send it out. But since they're used to free stuff, they may not actually buy anything. I may only get 100 sales of a book if I tried to charge for it. And I'm paying a lot of money to Mailchimp for my email list ($250 a month or so, but that's for the 56,732 subscribers I have in total).

So is it worth it to have a big list? I can set up a new giveaway where people have to Tweet about my book launch to enter. And I can get 1000 people to share and Tweet my message to their friends. And since my list is highly targeted (young adult readers, who enjoy similar books to mine) that's pretty great exposure. Even if I can *only* get 100 sales on launch, that's still pretty great. 100 sales is actually the amount of books I'm going to recommend you shoot for when you're starting out. And it's not the *only* thing I use my list for. In addition to the big list I've built using giveaways, I try to get people to join my actual fans list after they've read my fiction. That one is up to 4,175 subscribers, has a 29.1% open rate and a 7.6% click rate. Those are my beta readers. I'll send them an ARC copy a few weeks before launch and try to get 100 reviews in the first week, which of course will significantly boost sales and conversion.

So my lists are to help me get visibility and increase conversion on Amazon, and to help me spread the word about book launches. But my *income* comes from new readers discovering my books on Amazon for the first time and paying for them. That said, I no longer spend so much time and energy building my lists... I would like to get to 100K subscribers, just because it sounds awesome, and can be an influential marker of success. And I'd like to get a publishing deal later, and leading with the size of my email list and social media followers will help. While it won't convince an agent or publisher on its own, having a big following will motivate them to give my manuscript their full consideration.

But otherwise, what I should be doing is pruning my list and getting rid of everyone who hasn't opened my last 10 emails. That way I can keep my lists small and active, pay less in monthly fees, and still get the same amount of clicks. I know people who do really well with a small list of under a thousand, because those fans are highly engaged and eager to help promote. That comes from building a relationship with readers, which you can do through social media, by sending out interesting emails or an autoresponder series. I didn't plan to include this, but here are some brief suggestions for an autoresponder sequence.

- Thank them for signing up and give them the free book you promised.
- Ask them what their favorite book is and to introduce themselves on your Facebook page so you can get to know them.
- Ask them what their favorite character is and why, or what attributes they like in a main character.
- Do book reviews of the top 10 books in your genre (make a post and share it with them, also share it with the authors). Ask them to comment on which ones they read and liked the most (the other authors will see the engagement and be more likely to share).
- Do a monthly / quarterly post about best new releases in your field or genre.
- Tell an embarrassing story about yourself that connects with why you became a writer (include embarrassing pictures if possible – you're trying to be authentic and relatable)

- Remind them you share more giveaways on your Facebook page so they should follow you there to win more free books (then you can just share other people's giveaways, which is good content for your readers and also helps support other authors in your genre).
- Share long excerpts of the next book in the series, reminding them to pick it up or preorder if they haven't already.
- Share an exclusive story, with a new chapter each week (maybe put it on Wattpad and direct them there)

Wait, but how do you actually build a huge email list?
I mostly used a combination of book giveaways and Facebook ads.

You can use Rafflecopter, or Gleam, or Kingsumo for giveaways. I prefer Kingsumo for collecting emails, and Gleam for getting people to do specific tasks, like follow me on social media, Tweet or share something, or take some action like commenting on a post. I generally do a big Kingsumo giveaway to build a list, and then do a Gleam giveaway for the other things.

Here's my basic process: set up a page of my "10 favorite books in x genre." Get it in front of the authors so they can share it. Possibly also, at the same time, set up a giveaway of those ten books. Then I might email or message the authors and say, "Just wanted to let you know I featured your book in my list of 10 favorite books in X running a giveaway right now so I hope you visibility!" This will be easier if you have alr a relationship with the author, but still it's usually better to ask than not to (sometimes I don't reach out to the bigger authors because I don't think they'll reply, but actually when I tag them on Twitter, a lot of them share it).

My big win this year was getting Lauren Kate (author of *Fallen*) to share one of my giveaways, which I set up specifically as a celebration for the *Fallen* movie. She asked on Facebook what people were wearing to the movie premiere. I commented that we were giving away a pair of black feather wings and posted a link to the giveaway, which was titled *"28 amazing dark fantasy and supernatural thriller books for Fallen fans!"* She shared it on Twitter and Facebook to her 300K+ fans, and I got to tell all the authors I'd included that we got featured on Lauren Kate's page.

You *can* set up a multi-author giveaway and get all the authors to share it, and that works, but it's much easier to do everything yourself and just pay for Facebook ads. A lot of people are running list-building giveaways now, but most of them involve all the authors pitching in cash for prizes or a free Kindle. Firstly, that takes a lot of work and organization. Secondly, if you're sending out the new email list to all of the authors, the readers who opted in are going to get annoyed with all the emails, and won't be eager to sign up for a future giveaway. You can avoid this by telling authors what kind of content to send at first... I would basically say "most of the authors have at least one free book available, so even if you don't win, they'll be emailing soon to offer you their free book." You don't want 20+ authors mailing at the same time with promotional, salesy emails about their books.

I prefer to run everything myself because I like to keep control, it's a lot faster and easier for me to just set up myself, and I get to structure the way I build relationships with the new subscribers. You don't *need* to ask permission to buy and give away someone else's books, but it's generally a good idea to include them, because you want to be building relationships with those authors anyway. But since I've already built my post on my "favorite 10 books," after the giveaway I can just email everyone and send them to that post, or make a new post with links to everyone's websites or free book offer. I want to make sure I'm supporting, driving traffic and visibility, and benefiting all the authors involved, not just using their name or platform to market my own books.

★ Most people think of listbuilding as something that happens after you get people to your website, with an optin offer. That can work too, but that's usually something you offer from the back of your book, so that when they finish reading they go back to your site and sign up for something else. That's a different part of the process. It's important, but you still need to get people on your site. I do that with permafree books, but if you don't have permafree books, you need a lot of content, or advertising, and it still won't work nearly as well as book giveaways. If you need ideas though, here are <u>10 excellent optin offers fiction writers can use to build their emails lists.</u> Non-fiction should be even easier – just a free roadmap, listicle, cheat sheet, etc.

USE TWITTER AND FACEBOOK
TO FIND YOUR READERS

If you have your giveaway set up, you can run targeted Facebook ads to put it in front of the right readers. Facebook ads are super because you can narrow the interests and get very precise in your targeting. It's very difficult to get them to pay for a *single book* that you're trying to sell, though you can use them to promote the first in a series – or if you have lots of books, you can advertise a few of them to get people into your funnel, where you can recommend more books. Mark Dawson has made himself the king of Facebook ads for books, with good reason (last I checked he was making at least half a million dollars per year on his fiction). I believe he mostly runs ads to his free starter library to get people onto his list, then encourages them to buy more books in the series. Most of the time, advertising books when you only have one or two, will not achieve positive (profitable) results. However, you *do* want to launch each book as well as you can, so it can be very worthwhile to build up a big email list before your book launches, because it'll make it so much easier to get reviews and make your book "stick" for longer on Amazon. I'm not very careful with my ads, because they work well enough and I'm happy with the money I've spent. But if you were running continuous ads to promote a book, you'd need to tweak and perfect your ads until they were actually profitable (which is another nice thing about Facebook ads – you can see a lot of information and keep track of what's working).

Generally, you can start out in the Facebook ads manager and set up a custom audience, by targeting keywords related to your book (they'll be the same authors, books, keywords and categories you researched before). Previously, these keywords would all be "either/or" – so anybody who liked any of the keywords would see your advertisement. In 2016 however, Facebook introduced narrowed interests, so you can click on "narrow further" and select more keywords for more specific targeting. Instead of people who like mermaids OR young adult fiction OR the Twilight series, now I can target people who like all three. Then I can speak directly to them with my ad copy, like "This thrilling new young adult novel is being compared to Twilight... with mermaids. Get your copy now!"

I prefer to narrow interests until my target audience is really small, maybe less than 20,000. But you can also test with bigger, broader audiences and see what happens. Just don't overspend: be careful not to set an ad to run indefinitely (I spent almost $1000 once before I realized I'd left an ad running). Start small, for $5 or $10 a day and measure the results. If people aren't clicking your ad, make it better. If people *are* clicking your ad, but not buying the book or signing up to your list, there's a problem with your sales or landing page you need to fix. Facebook ads are also great for figuring out where your problems are... you can test covers and ad copy until people are clicking *and* buying.

Once you've set up an audience in Facebook ads, you can also choose that audience when you use boosted posts. Generally, boosted posts don't perform as well. You may get *engagements* without getting clicks (people can like or share or comment, without actually clicking). But I use them because they're easy. Just try to encourage engagement and action by being specific about what you want them to do: "Sign up to win! First, click the link and sign up, then share with your friends." I'll also try to ask them questions, like "which of these books have you read?" because the more comments I get, the less Facebook charges me to share that content to new readers. I also like boosted posts because, when I boost a book giveaway, a lot of people will *also* like my Facebook page. My Urban Epics Facebook group has 5,987 likes. Rather than setting up an author page for myself, I set up a genre-based group, which is less personal but easier to get people to like and support, so it grows faster.

With both groups and pages, the real problem is that organic reach is very low. You can increase it by posting engaging content, but you'll still have trouble reaching most of your followers. I still appreciate Facebook and social media followers for social proof (people see how many followers you have and attach credibility based on your numbers). It's not the only thing that matters, but it's a small thing that can help you get over that initial resistance whenever you meet someone new, whether a fellow author you're trying to make friends with or a potential reader. For me, anything less than 1000 followers is a little risky; you can overcome it by being awesome and confident and just showing up, but using the tactics I'm recommending, you can also get a bunch of followers quickly. With Kingsumo giveaways, you have the option for people to tag you on Twitter when they share the contest, so with a contest + boosted posts on Facebook + the Tweetstorm that results, I get a lot of subscribers, likes and followers.

Twitter has its own advertising system, which can be effective sometimes; you can also target by likes and interests or keywords. I just logged in, since it's been awhile actually and I wanted to see what's changed. Previously, Twitter wasn't so great with targeting so I haven't used it as much. Now though, you can build a "media studio" with all your graphics in a unified library, and you can choose between three "creatives" (Tweets, Cards, Media).

The cards are lead-generation cards, which means people can sign up for your offer right on Twitter (Facebook also has this, and I have friends who have gotten great results). I'd like to test both soon – basically you advertise your free book or offer to get them on your list, then try to get them to continue the series. The reason I haven't done a lot of these, is because I *don't have any series.* I'll definitely spend some money on lead generation in Twitter and Facebook later when I can see results. For now, I might use Twitter to put one of my giveaway Tweets in front of more readers.

Just for fun, I set up two ads on Twitter. I went under "Tweets" and "Organic Tweets" to choose two Tweets I want to promote; one is promoting the 99cent boxset I'm in, the other is for a $100 Amazon giveaway and author swag. People have to retweet the first promotional Tweet to enter.

So my promotional Tweet will get more shares, and people will see the giveaway and sign up to win, and retweet the promotional Tweet. Basically doubling up on the same thing. The boxset is #3,243 in the paid store right now. I'm going to spend $100 in 24 hours and see what happens.

First I had to go to "campaigns" and make a new campaign with specific objectives (website visits, followers, awareness or engagements). I chose website visits – I want them to click my link and leave Twitter. I found the advertising system confusing and a bit buggy, but managed to add my Tweet creatives to a campaign and get it running. They have TV targeting, which could be awesome for promoting genre fiction, but I couldn't get it working. Twitter says my $100 will only get about 150 clicks.

Results:

After a day, my two ads look like this (the top bar is combined results). I've gotten 307 clicks for $50, which means I'll probably get over 600 total. Way more than Twitter's estimates. And not bad results.

Impressions	Spend	Results	Results rate	Cost per result
8,176	$50.00	307 Link clicks	3.75% Link click rate	$0.16 Cost per link click
3,847	$24.19	152 Link clicks	3.95% Link click rate	$0.16 Cost per link click
4,329	$25.81	155 Link clicks	3.58% Link click rate	$0.17 Cost per link click

However, clicks don't equal purchases. In this case, I'm promoting giveaways that get people to share the 99cent book on Amazon, so I may see results for the next week. This kind of promotion *might* be valuable if you're doing a big free or 99cent campaign and need more sales and downloads. If you can spend $100, get 600 clicks and 50 sales, those extra 50 sales might be worthwhile, because they'd push you up higher on Amazon and get more visibility. And they *might* be fine if you're advertising a free book to get people to sign up to your list, and you have a big collection of books for them to buy. But generally, advertising on social media doesn't work, because:

Social media is not where people go to buy books. They will talk about books. They will pay attention to book reviews or mentions. They will like and share any cool book-related content. But they'll probably ignore (or be annoyed by) any outright ads asking them to buy something. This is why I almost never promote my books on social media; I don't run a lot of ads for paid books; I don't use lots of exclamation points because the book is "FREE!!!"

Actually I'll unfollow authors who post things like that, or share or retweet similar content. This is basically what I wrote against in *Book Marketing is Dead*. Social media is a place to be social, talk about things, share cool content and make friends. Not advertise. It might work, a little, anyway – but you're *interrupting* the normal content that they are there to consume and trying to distract them with something else they aren't expecting, which isn't going to work that well.

NATIVE CONTENT (WHY ADVERTISING FAILS)

It's no secret that advertising doesn't work that well anymore. People resent it. Or, maybe that's not exactly true, but let's say conversion is down. For many businesses, advertising doesn't work as well as it used to. People want truer, more authentic experiences. So the best way to reach customers is to put a piece of content into the platforms they're already using, without trying to make it into promotional copy or advertising. Just something fun and cool – something that fits in and belongs on that platform. A piece of content that "gets it" and knows the rules, so it doesn't seem like a dad just trying to be hip. This is referred to as *native content* (I probably heard the term from Gary Vaynerchuk).

At the movie theater recently I saw a pretty good example from M&Ms. There were a bunch of advertisements and movie premieres, but there was also that video they play to remind you to turn off your mobile phone.

Only that whole video was made by M&Ms. And it was actually an entertaining little script, with those M&M characters. It was a story. The story ended with a reminder to turn off your cell phone. It was an expected, normal part of the movie-going experience. Totally within the rules. If it wasn't M&M, something much lamer would have been there. But it was also providing value (retelling the boring rules in a fresh way and making it interesting). Of course it was covered in branding, the whole thing was a big ad, but it wasn't selling or suggesting you go buy some.

Instead it increases brand trust and loyalty, and makes people think good things about the company. They might think of M&Ms when they want to have a fun, family party. Because they associate M&Ms with color, entertainment and happiness. M&Ms could have just taken out an ad. I don't know how much they had to pay to get featured like that. Maybe nothing. The movie theater has to play something there. If M&Ms provides a really cool clip that movie goers enjoy, why not play it? M&Ms created something useful and essential, that theaters could actually use. Maybe they distributed it for free and are getting free advertising out of it. I don't know.

The point is, you should be looking for things like that. Things that are out there, being done, necessary, common, but boring... and redo them. Make them better. For example, sometimes when I see a blogger I follow say something cool or post a great manifesto, I'll turn it into an image quote or infographic. They'll share it with their audience, and usually credit me. All I'm doing is making them look good. Win-win. If someone is looking for a logo or header or seal or something, maybe I can spend 10 minutes and make something for them. Maybe they'll use it and link back to me in the credits. My point is, **don't make advertising, make value.**

Make lots of value for people with big platforms, or something that will be liked, enjoyed, shared. Give value to make your brand stronger and get people aware of who you are and what you do. It works better than advertising (in some cases). Advertising has a role too, and can be very successful. Advertising belongs where advertising is... but native content, cool stuff that doesn't look like advertising, can often reach far more people on a much smaller budget.

AMAZON ADS

So am I saying not to advertise? No – only that, if you're going to advertise, you want adverts that blend in and catch readers at the right time... when they're actually looking for new books to buy. That's what makes AMS (Amazon Marketing Services) so powerful. I'll admit, I'm pretty new at using AMS, but after seeing a few indie authors explode their sales, I've been testing it out recently with great results.

Here's how it works: in the KDP dashboard, you can click on a book and go to "promote and advertise." Then set up an ad. You can choose "Sponsored Products," or "Product Display Ads." Sponsored products tend to show up right under the search results and *look like* normal search results if you aren't paying attention. So they blend in.

That's what I use, but you can try out product display ads as well if you want to.

Choose the book you want to advertise and set a daily budget (I recommend setting an end date so you don't forget to turn it off. After the first round is over, you can make a copy of the ad and try again.) Then you choose your keywords. You want to target authors and books that are similar to yours. You can use the list you made earlier, but I would expand it. While I'm still experimenting, the strategy I've heard works best is choosing at least 100 keywords to start off, then removing all the ones that aren't performing well.

Once your ad campaign gets going, your book will start showing up when people search for those keywords. So my mermaid book will be more likely to show up when people search for "mermaids." The first time I ran the ad, I mostly used other mermaid books or authors that had written mermaid books. The problem is, mermaids aren't a hugely popular category. Unlike some other advertising platforms, it can be hard to get Amazon to take your money at first. I tried to spend $5 a day, but there weren't enough people searching for the keywords I chose, so actually the campaign ended when I'd only spent $3.27.

For that $3.27, however, I got 33 clicks and *one sale at $3.99*. Which is actually great. Amazon also keeps track of your ACoS, or "average cost per sale." It cost me $3.27 to make $3.99, so mine was 81.95%. That means, in theory, I could spend $327 and make $399. The problem was, I didn't use enough keywords that people were searching for. So I just redid the ad, this time, I tried to write better sales copy (you get one short line of description, you need a powerful hook). I also added in *tons* of keywords. Instead of just targeting mermaid books, I branched out and included all the major young adult bestselling books and authors that were marginally similar to mine. The thing is, you have to show up, and then your ad has to convert. If they like the book, they'll be happy. They won't know or care why the book showed up when they were searching for something else; as long as it got their attention and they enjoyed it.

But here's the other thing: I also ran a campaign for *Scarlet Thread*, one of my other novels. In this case, my ACoS was 173.19%. I spent $113.77, got 503 clicks, and made $65.69. On the surface, I lost money. But actually, those sales kept my rank up higher, which got me more sales and lots of page reads (I'll make about $1000 this month from that one book). Also, it was priced at 99cents, so it's much more difficult to see an actual return on investment from the ads; I could raise it to $2.99 and keep fiddling with my ads, but right now the advertising campaign stopped and it's still holding a really strong rank (about #2500), so it's easier/cheaper for me to leave it at 99cents and keep earning $1000 a month, rather than spend $5 a day in ads and trying to earn more (but that's the kind of thing you'd want to test out... which way makes more money?)

Here's the really exciting thing: if you start with even $3 a day, you can keep tweaking your ads until they perform well. Ideally you'll remove any keywords that aren't working and try some more, until you have a bunch of keywords that work and are getting an ACoS rate of under 100%. If you can do that, you can just keep spending more money. As long as you're breaking even or better, you can dump money into the system. It's basically free marketing (as long as you're earning it back), it takes very little upkeep or organization, and it's extremely powerful. Amazon ads even seem to have learning abilities; they get better with time. Remember, Amazon *wants* to show your book to the right readers and get sales – that's how Amazon makes its money.

ALSO BOUGHTS

Amazon (and other online retailers) will show a *customers who bought this book have also bought...* section. You want your book to show up in the other bestselling books in your genre. There are several ways to do that:

- You can encourage readers who bought your book to also buy the other books you want to be associated with – for example you can send them back to your "top 10 books in X genre" post.
- You can get those authors to send their fans to you, by giving away or supporting their books or by making friends with them (good long-term strategy, but slow).
- You can use advertising to target those books and authors, until your book starts showing up in their also-boughts (fastest and easiest).

While you can use Amazon ads long-term to keep your rank high, I don't think you have to. What I'm going to start doing, is spending $100 a day on Amazon ads during launch week. Basically, I want very specific people to be buying my books, so my also-boughts stay "clean." The problem with "shotgun" marketing like email or Twitter blasts is that you might get a bunch of random people who don't actually read your genre. By spending on Amazon ads, rank will stay high during launch week, *and* you should improve your also-boughts section. You could just spend $5 a day for a few months while the book is on pre-order, and I may try this too, but now that I know what I'm doing I want my books to do really well on launch and keep selling long term.

So *besides* all the normal book-launch strategies I've been using, I'll also focus on Amazon ads. I'll generally start cheap and play with things while the book is on preorder, until hopefully I can get my ACoS to under 100% - then I can spend $100 a day for 10 days during launch, and be pretty confident that I'll earn all that money back in book sales (actually I'll probably make at least double: from the page reads, and also from all the extra sales that come from the increase in visibility).

HOW TO GET A HUNDRED REVIEWS IN ONE WEEK

One of the big problems with launching a book, is that you can't really promote it without reviews. Some of the big advertising sites have a minimum of five or ten reviews, and even if they didn't, your promotions won't be very successful without reviews. (Readers may not even buy it with a bunch of positive reviews – they want to see a spread of mixed reviews, even some negative ones, which makes them all more believable.) But how do you get them?

One way is to reach out to lots of reviewers, bloggers, other authors, websites and anyone else you can think of. I did that for my first book and got some great reviews from leading magazines. But now, years later, that book still has less than 50 reviews total. Another way is to ask all your friends and family to post reviews. I don't do that. It puts them in an awkward situation. Even if they loved the book, some people just aren't comfortable writing reviews. One thing you *can* do is look on Amazon, write down all the reviewers who reviewed books similar to yours, and see if you can find a blog or contact info – then send them a copy.

Recently I used a service called BookRazor to collect this info for me. They built an email list for me of reviewers – these are readers that are likely to *also* review books, so they're great leads. I emailed them a free book; I was worried about it because I don't like reaching out to strangers, but the majority of them were happy to get a free book and promised to review when they had time. If you're cold-emailing this way, you might want to send once, send again to the non-opens, check back in a week to see if they got the email, and then follow up a month later if they haven't reviewed it yet. But that's a lot of work; I just emailed them once.

What I much prefer to do instead, is run my book giveaways and build a huge list of readers, and then offer them an ARC copy. You can use BookFunnel or InstaFreebie to host your free book in multiple formats. Even if you're going into KU, you can put up an ARC copy of the book out for readers before you launch (but you can't keep making it available after). B
just a place to host the book files, and lets yc

many copies you're giving away. InstaFreebie actually has its own readership, so you can put a book there and often get 1000 subscribers without really doing anything. In the future, I'll probably offer a limited amount of ARC copies for review, and email my list telling them they can get one *if* they have time to read it quickly and leave a review in the first week, and that everyone else can get the book for free when it launches (when you're in KU, you have a few free days you can use. I'll usually use one right away, for my list to download the book for free, because I know I'll get lots of reviews that way... then I'll use the rest later to connect with new readers).

If your book is on preorder, you can put up the print version and make it unavailable, so people can start posting reviews early (if so, send out review copies several weeks in advance). If not, you probably need to do a soft launch, wait for some reviews to be posted, then do a hard launch with ads in about a week. You don't really need 100 reviews, but I'd recommend getting at least 10 before you start marketing (and not all positive ones – don't worry about it if somebody on your betareader list gives your book a bad review. I would take them off your list, since they don't enjoy your writing, but a critical, negative review will often boost sales, as long as they don't lambast you for issues readers feel strongly about).

I put up an ARC version several weeks early, make the paperback version as soon as possible, hopefully before the book launches, then email people who got a copy of the book early and remind them to review it as soon as possible. You *can* offer postcards or something as a thank you for your readers, but be careful you're not giving things away *in exchange for* a book review. The free ebooks I'm sending out aren't really *in exchange* for reviews – I give out copies for free to my fans to thank them for supporting me, and I hope they review, but it's not a condition (I don't say they *have* to. And I'd never expect a *positive* review).

The other big trick I've used is simply leaving a book on permafree for several months. It's easy, you'll get a lot of reviews, and you can set it back to paid later (I usually wait till I have over 100 reviews). All of these tactics can be used to get 100 reviews in a week, but you do need to follow up and nag a little bit if you really want to make it happen; plus having that big email list really helps, so get started on that.

★ **Should you pay for reviews?** I don't think so. Obviously, you should never pay for fake reviews, or do anything to try and mislead readers. But many authors pay hundreds of dollars for reviews from reputable review sites like Kirkus or Foreword. I don't think those are necessary, and the money could be better spent on ads or promotion.

HOW TO SELL 100 COPIES ON LAUNCH DAY AND HIT #1

So the day has come. You've got at least 10 reviews. You've been testing ad copy (Facebook and Amazon ads are a great way to fine-tune your hook and pitch). As I mentioned, I usually do a "soft launch" first, which means when the book is live I don't actually tell many people about it. I use my KDP Select free days, probably just one to reward my followers and to generate more reviews, then will set the price to $2.99 or $3.99 for about a week while reviews trickle in.

Then I'll do a "hard launch" where I try to spike the rank with sales. The thing about sales is, generally you can get more downloads if the book is discounted. So you do a 99cent promotion, and advertise or share it. This is also because, a lot of the "cheap book" promotional sites are more interested in sharing deals, not books at full price.

I think you should shoot for 100 sales on launch day (the day that you've decided to push hard and boost your rank). That's usually enough to get you near the top #1000 on Amazon, and probably #1 in your category, as long as you've chosen categories well and are in some less competitive ones. Generally, the way to do a 99cent campaign is to ask all your friends to share and support it. I don't like to do that. More recently, I've been setting up giveaways where, to enter, they need to Tweet the 99cent book deal. That way I can get my list to share the 99cent book (even though they've probably already gotten the free book).

I used to try Facebook ads for the 99cent book deal but they didn't work that well and it was hard to boost the rank up. Now, I'll mostly use Amazon ads, but I'll also promote on some 99cent book deal sites. Most of them charge a fee to share your discounted book with their email list. Sales will depend on your book cover, your hook or description, and your Amazon page and reviews – so again, make sure all of that stuff is really tight before you spend money on promotion.

You usually want to make more money than you spend, but on your big launch, I would say it's OK to go big. Use most of your budget and try to push that rank up as high as you can.

Some people like to use a ThunderClap campaign or something similar to get the word out: those websites let people sign up to share a promotional message at the same time. I tried that for my first fiction book launch, and it didn't go so well (even though, according to them, we had a reach of over a million people). This is mostly because, as I've noted, promotion on social media doesn't work that well anyway. I tried to be clever, by donating the money I made for my mermaid book to save manatee, and getting some oceanic conservation groups to share it. Might have been good for visibility and brand awareness, but not great for sales. But also, if I'm going to ask people to do one thing, I think it's a waste to get them to share a ThunderClap, I'd rather have them join my list, or download my book (I also wouldn't keep promoting the same book to the same audience over and over again. Put it in front of them, but in a non-promotional, indirect way).

One of the reasons it's been hard for me to get lots of sales on launch, however, is that I'm giving my book away for free to my list. You don't *have* to do that. You can just launch at $2.99 and keep it there if you want to, and see whether anybody on that big email list you built will buy it. But generally, for the *first book* especially, you'll be asking people to take a risk on whether they will like your writing, and conversion will be low. I prefer to give out free books to prove my value and get fans eager for more.

For my next big book launch, I'll probably give out ARC copies (but a limited amount), then a 99cent promotion on launch, but save the free days for a few weeks later. Then I can tell my list, "You can still get it for free, if you want to wait... or you can grab it for 99cents now and start reading!" Eventually, I won't give all my books for free, and I'll just launch paid books. But I'll be able to do that because I've built a strong and passionate platform. I hear a lot of authors talking about how cheap and free books "devalue" literature, and they've worked long and hard on their books and they deserve to get paid.

My response: your book has zero value if you can't get anyone to buy it. So if you keep your book at $3.99 but only sell 20 copies a month, you're both cheating yourself of the money you could be earning by using my tactics, and cheating all the fans that will never read your book because you haven't made it accessible to them. It's not your fans job to "support literature" by paying for a book they don't want. It's your job to convince them of the value of your work. And with so much competition free books are a simple and easy (not to mention *free*) way to get ahead of all the noise and be seen.

But also: like I said, I used to think $2.99 is a good price, and that you should do 99cent promos every month or two to boost rank and get more readers. Right now I'm less sure. That's because, at 99cents my books have a lower sales rank and *earn more money* with page reads. If I raise the price to 2.99, my rank isn't as good and my earnings go down. Also, I think I'll probably stick more with Amazon ads and less with all the promotional sites, so I don't really need to worry about making the book look like a deal or bargain by being discounted.

BE INCLUSIVE

I added this section in late but it's important, especially for non-fiction. The easy way to have a bestselling book is to include lots of other people in it. For example, what I *could have* done is quote 100 bloggers who talk about book marketing and include them in this book, then tell them I've featured them. They will be likely to share it on launch. I've done that for some of my earlier books, and I'll do it for later books, but I didn't for this one. It's also a really easy way to write a non-fiction book: you just pick a topic, research 100 people talking about the topic, send them a simple form, ask them to tell a personal story or give their top tip, feature them and then let them know when the book is available (it's a little weird to ask them to share a paid book, which is another reason why starting with a free campaign wins – they're likely to share your book with their audience as long as it's free for a limited time).

They get to be included in your project, which makes them look good. I'd probably also make a big post linking to all of their websites, which is free marketing for them. You can check out an example of that in this post: <u>61 brilliant publishing tips from industry insiders on how to write, publish and promote your book.</u>

I talked about publishing on a cruise ship recently with over one hundred digital nomads (people who work online and can travel full-time). I was talking about writing non-fiction to build your platform, and I said there were basically two kinds of books: the simple, practical, no-nonsense guides that prove you're an expert, and the personal branding books that are more about you and what you hope to achieve in your business.

For the majority of non-fiction books, you need to blend content and information with *story,* but it doesn't have to be *your story.* Writing a book is actually a brilliant way to network with the leaders in your field, because all you have to do is pick a topic and ask them to contribute. Make it simple and easy for them, don't send a huge form. Get a beautiful cover first so they can see it's a project they're comfortable being included in. It'll take 10 minutes for them to write a paragraph or two, either a tip or a story (if you have multiple topics throughout several chapters, you could have them choose ANY topic and write one tip and one story.)

Then you just need to try and organize things all together. You want your book to be entertaining, which is why story is important, but you also want it to be educational and useful (so people get real benefits and take action). And you don't want it to just be a dump of stories or tips, you want to organize it coherently (although some authors like Steve Scott have done tremendously well with books that are broken down into many small tips or topics).

It's a little harder for fiction, but one way I do this is by offering a post of recommended other books in the back of mine. So at the end of Shearwater, I have a list of "30 other amazing mermaid books you'll love" or something like that; which goes to my blog post of great mermaid books. I can tell the authors I've featured that post inside my book, and even if I don't do that, they're likely to share my article; and sending people to that post will also improve my also-boughts. The point is, try to include other people in your book somehow. Give them a reason to share and help you promote it, if you can.

★ For this book, I'll probably reach out to all the tools or people I've mentioned just to let them know I said nice things about them.

HOW TO SELL 1000 COPIES A WEEK WITH AD-STACKING

I think I first heard the term "ad-stacking" from Joanna Penn, though I've seen the strategy used before that. Basically, instead of just signing up for a handful of the book promotion sites, you sign up for *lots* of them, and you spread them out during launch week, so you have two or three promos a day. That way, instead of one big push on day one, you get continued sales for about a week – proving to Amazon you aren't just doing one big blast. It's *likely* that this will help keep your rank more stable long term.

This is the launch strategy I mapped out for my big launch of Shearwater a few months ago... six days of big promotions. Each site has different prices depending on the genre and whether it's free or paid. BookBub is far more expensive (and far more effective) than all the others. All together this would probably cost around $1000 to s⁄ but you could just pick 5 of them and get it down t $200.

Day 1: BookBub, GenrePulse, Booksends, Jus⁄

Day 2: BookZio, eReaderNewsToday, Reading Deals, BookSends, Read Cheaply
Day 3: Bargain Booksy, Booktastik, Books Butterfly, Free Kindle Books and Tips
Day 4: Kindle Nation Daily, Book Gorilla, eBookSoda
Day 5: Reading Deals, Book Lemur, Ask David
Day 6: The Fussy Librarian, Robin Reads, Book Barbarian

And while this strategy *works* I also think it's short-sighted. In general, you'll get 10x more free downloads than sales of even a 99cent book – so as long as you're paying to reach other people's lists, what you really want is for them to sign up on *your list* so you don't need to keep paying to access other people's audiences. (Plus, getting lots of random readers to buy your book will spike your rank, but can mess up your also-boughts section, which is important for long-term sales).

So especially if you haven't built a big platform yet, and plan to write lots of books and series, I would actually do a huge free campaign, advertise with all of those sites, and try to get people to read + enjoy + sign up on your website for bonus content. You need a really strong offer; I usually say "get the next book for free." I've seen authors do a great launch strategy and sell a lot of books with ad-stacking, and then spend the next year trying to get their rank up higher with lots of little marketing tactics that aren't really doing anything. In contrast, I gave away *Scarlet Thread* for six months, got 186 reviews, and now it stays at #1 in two categories, with a strong sales rank, with zero promotion or advertising, and earns consistent revenue.

THE BEST FREE AND PAID PROMOTION SITES

I think things are constantly changing, and it's probably not fair to single out the "best" promotion sites, but these are the ones that seem to perform the best for me – for young adult fantasy.

FreeBooksy, ENT, AskDavid.com, Book Barbarian, Robin Reads, Choosy Bookworm.

So if you're on a budget and want results, I'd start with those. BookBub, however, is the King Kong of book promotion sites. There are different strategies on how to get accepted for a BookBub ad, but things seem pretty random. The cover helps a lot; the number and quality of reviews, but also what days you're applying for and what other promotions are scheduled for those days. The best advice is to keep trying, maybe once a month, changing up how you pitch the book (you're allowed to add in some extra comments). You may want to note how many reviews you have on GoodReads and Amazon, or any other important info that might help them make a decision. I've seen them feature permafree books, and boxsets, first in a series... BookBub ads are expensive but will usually earn well.

I won't pursue them seriously however until I have a full series up and lots more books (everything you do has more impact if you have more books out). So I'm still kind of playing around for now until I can produce more work, then I'll start ramping up my advertising budget, because it'll be easier for me to at least break even with my ads. (If you can break even with your ads, that means you'r advertising for free, and can basically spend an infinite amount of resources to push your book to the top of the bestseller lists.)

For free book promotions, I often use KDRoi, Book Marketing Tools or a cheap Fiverr.com gig to list my book to dozens of promo sites. For 99cent campaigns, I'd be more choosy and try to submit to the big ones I want individually. There are also a lot of Facebook groups and Reddit pages for free books, but I'm not sure how effective they are (still, every bit helps, and posting probably can't hurt.)

AMAZON GIVEAWAYS

There are some other tricks you can use that *might* help you sell your 100 books and boost your sales rank. One of them is Amazon Giveaways. Once your book is live, you can give away a certain number of your books; people can enter by following you on Amazon or Twitter. There's no way to see *how many* people are following you on Amazon, but having lots of followers can be really effective: they'll see when you put a new book out and Amazon will often email them about it. Plus, when you give away those books, ⸱he winners have to go and claim their copy, and that ⸱ld count as a sale and boost your rank a little (I'm still ⸱nting with this, results are mixed, it doesn't seem ⸱k as quickly as a normal sale but still seems to

instead of making my book free and ⸱ay, I could give away 100 copies ⸱ get the added benefit of the follows, and those 100 copies might help boost rank. Likewise, you can "gift" a copy of your book on Amazon to anyone with an email address. But this way you need to manually gift out all the copies (with Amazon Giveaways it's more automatic and easier). Gifted copies, if claimed, should also boost rank. I'd like to experiment more with both, in larger numbers, to see if I can measure the results.

Another thing you can do though, that's a little bit sneaky, is set up Amazon giveaways for *other books* in your genre. So instead of getting KingSumo or one of the other giveaway plugins, you can just set up Amazon giveaways to get followers. For example if I wrote science fiction thrillers, I could give away Stephen King books and get people to follow me, then boost that giveaway on Facebook to fans of Stephen King. That may not work that well, because readers may feel duped, but you can just as easily give away a free Kindle or something really cool that only appeals to your target readership.

This year I'll focus on building up my Amazon followers, and also my BookBub followers, using giveaways (under the hypothesis that having more BookBub followers makes it easier to get accepted for ad campaigns, which may not be true).

NEWSLETTER SWAPS

2016 was my first year of publishing fiction – so I concentrated on building a big list and was very careful with what I shared. However, now that I'm focused on my books generating income, I'm prepared to promote other (talented) authors in my genre to my list, in exchange with them promoting my books to their list.

This is typically called a "newsletter swap." I've avoided these in the past. I don't like recommending anything I haven't read, and I don't like the idea of exchanging help or promotion. I'd rather get people to share or promote because they want to, not because they must. That said, newsletter swaps can be very effective, for a variety of reasons.

I heard someone say on Facebook recently that your list isn't just about promoting you and your books; it also represents value to the other authors in your community. One of the reasons I like having a big list isn't just because it makes it easier to market my own books, but because I can have a significant boost to other authors in my genre.

Generally, however, you try trading with someone of about the same list size... on Facebook groups you can sometimes offer a list swap, or if you're doing a launch or 99cent/free promotion you can ask people to share it in their newsletters and you'll share theirs when they have a launch. For someone like me though, who is pretty bad at staying organized and doesn't send emails on any kind of consistent schedule, keeping track of who I'm supposed to be promoting has been a chore.

Recently I found Newsletter Swap, and I've been enjoying it. Authors can list their books, the dates they'd like to 1 romoted, and apply to swap. The really great h, besides keeping things organized and u when you need to send an email, is you special link that keeps track of clicks. That about the list size, because people can see the number of actual clicks you get. This also makes things more like a game – the transparency encourages me to work harder to get more clicks for the authors I've swapped with.

Besides the simple and obvious benefits of an email list trade, the other thing I like is that it lets me connect with other authors in my genre who are looking for promotion and really focus on getting them some sales. It's their first interaction with me, and I want to make it positive and provide results. You're only supposed to accept three books at a time on the Newsletter Swap site, but recently I accepted nine.

I set up a very simple email, without the book description, and asked people to click on the covers to learn more (which I believe will result in more clicks for more books – getting them to the Amazon page is a bigger win than losing them immediately if the summary didn't grab them).

Then I made a quick post on my blog, "Some Great New Reads for January!" then I posted that on my Facebook group and spent $15 to promote it with my audience... and then I wrote a post about it on my main blog, which will get the authors some long-term visibility. This was really easy to do, and took me about 20 minutes + $15.

Like I said, I want results, so the authors can see I'm actually promoting them and going the extra mile to get them some traffic. So far, I've gotten over 100 clicks per book. I can't tell how many sales that is, maybe not that many, but at least they're getting visibility (and I have seen the rank drop on most of them, though I'm sure the authors are doing lots of other promotion right now for their sale).

<u>Newsletter Swap</u> is new, so it will be more powerful once more authors start using it, but I really like the idea. It may also help you with the issue of "what do I email my list about?" You want to send them something, at least twice a month or so. Ideally you'd share cheap or free books in your genre, but it could also be book recommendations. I started the Alliance of Young Adult Authors group in part so that we can share our book launch information; we keep a big list of dates and new titles, that way we always have content to email our lists about if we want to. You could also just get a virtual assistant to find 10 new releases in your genre, make a nice-looking blog post about it with links to the books, email your list about it (to send more traffic to your site + if you use Amazon affiliate links you can earn some money + to let your readers know you're connected with the genre they love and focused on introducing them to great new reads). Then you can send that post to all the authors and let them know you've featured them and emailed your list. I don't typically ask for anything in exchange... but I may hope we become friends on Facebook, and that they may share my book launches when they see them *because they want to.*

INCENTIVES FOR BULK ORDERS

Most of the things I do, I realize, are small time tactics. I recommend them, because they are pretty easy to pull off without a large budget or platform. I have indie author friends who make $50K a month on book sales, and think if a book isn't making over $500 a month it's "failing." They focus on producing more books and quick wins – simple things that gets lots of sales.

I also have friends that have built million-dollar businesses by having meticulously crafted, polished content. Beautiful websites, high quality book production, professional headshots and everything else. The danger, I think, is trying to immediately match everything those people are doing from day one, without a platform. Also, doing a huge book launch with lots of incentives for bulk orders may *work* but will cost a lot, and probably won't earn very much immediately (sales will come later, after you've hit bestseller lists or gotten a ton of promotion). These campaigns usually also rely on some kind of a business funnel that includes courses, services or high-priced digital products or live events. So authors can *lose money* on the book but still make money on everything else.

If you're just starting out with no platform, doing something like this could be risky, especially if you don't have any way to make money from the book other than actual book sales. But because it *can be* really successful, here are some ways I would do it.

Fiction: I was hoping to have my mermaid book out before Christmas. That way, I could say "if you buy 5 books, I'll send you a free mermaid-tail blanket." Readers could probably think of 5 people to give the book away to near the holidays, and they'd also earn a mermaid blanket for themselves or as a gift. One easy decision that would take care of a lot of shopping. The trick is to calculate how much money you'd need to buy the prizes (including shipping) to make sure you have enough. But the point isn't to earn money, it's to break even and boost your sales rank.

You can also do this on a smaller scale; buy or preorder the book and send them something cute, simple and cheap... I've gotten mermaid pendants from Etsy, jewelry, posters or postcards, or other cool things.

You can also offer a bigger prize for preorders or book orders on launch; where they need to purchase the book, then enter a contest and add their purchase confirmation number. Technically, in the USA (as I understand it), a giveaway where purchase is required is illegal – so you'd need to have an option for entering for free, but they could earn more entries by also buying the book.

I was planning on giving away a free trip to Ireland to see all the places mentioned in the novel, but didn't finish the book in time (spent a lovely month in Ireland writing, though). You can get creative with prizes to encourage orders, but try to keep things as simple as possible – for example it's easier to just order something online and ship it directly to winners rather than mailing everything yourself.

Non-fiction: This strategy usually works a little better with non-fiction. I haven't really planned out a launch campaign for this book yet (*Guerrilla Publishing*), but some things I could do are:

- Order 5 books and get a free website review ($100 value)
- Order 10 books and get the companion course for free ($349 value)

- Order 25 books for a one-hour coaching session ($500 value)
- Order 50 books and I'll speak at your conference ($1000 value)

These are just samples, but you get the idea.

This only works with print books, since you can't order multiple copies of ebooks. I already have some permafree books, so I'll probably price this one at $2.99 and run constant Amazon ads to keep the rank high, rather than doing a huge launch campaign. I may also set up a landing page and use Facebook ads to promote this book for free, to get people into an email funnel and encourage them to upgrade to a course or publishing package if they need more help or feedback.

I hope this book is *helpful* but I think it's probably also a little overwhelming, especially if you're not familiar with online marketing and advertising. I don't mind giving away all my secrets for free because I know most people are going to need more support. My courses include step-by-step videos on how to actually set up all the technical stuff, and getting some feedback from me personally will save dozens of frustrating hours trying to do it all yourself. (I basically only charge for things that take up my time; but I'm happy to share my knowledge for free).

CHALLENGE #3

Launch your book!

Post your results in the Guerrilla Publishing Facebook group.

Share your successes or any questions you have.

4: FAST GROWTH
FOR MORE SALES

INDIRECT MARKETING HACKS TO GET
MORE VISIBILITY WITHOUT BEING
AN ANNOYING SPAMMER

I'm leaving this section here because I like the title. Most people see "marketing" as "telling people about your book." And that's the problem. Most authors, even most author promotion services, are using spammy, shotgun tactics that don't work and probably also annoy people.

The solution is to *not talk about your book*. Talk about other people's books. Talk about things happening in your genre or field. Share interesting articles from other authors in your genre that you're following (if you aren't already, you should be following all the authors in your genre so you can share, like and comment on their content).

I actually hardly talk about my book launches at all on social media. I build lists, and I put together offers, and I let people know when things are available. If I share something on social media it will be a credibility booster, like "I just got my 100th review! Thanks everyone!" or "My new book hit #1 today! Thanks everyone who supported it – it's still 99cents for a few more hours."

Discounted pricing isn't *enough* to get a sale. Nor is telling people how hard you worked on it or asking them to support you (nobody owes you anything). People *do* like to buy books that are popular or successful, however. It's much more likely people will click your links if you're sharing the *success* of your book, and not just asking people for support. (In fact, these are usually the kinds of posts that I'll boost on Facebook, because they perform better than promotional stuff).

But you can also mention things in an indirect way. For example, when I redid my book covers, I asked people for feedback on the new covers. I'll do that again just before launch with a few color variations. When I was getting the audiobooks produced, I made a video of my top 5 narrators and asked people to comment on which voice they thought fit my character. That got lots of engagement.

You don't want to *tell* your audience things. You want to *ask* them things. You need to seduce by withdrawing and leaving a space for them to share something about themselves (I took that from my PhD Thesis on *Paradise Lost*). Don't try to sell your book to people. Try and get them involved in the process of your book, the story, the journey. Give them a sense of ownership by showing that you value their feedback. Use the book to build a relationship.

I also usually share all the book marketing hacks, strategies and case studies I'm doing on my websites. None of them are promotional, but the articles are still indirectly related to my books. If you don't have a big platform or much blog traffic, you can post things like this in Facebook groups, or even on Reddit (which is dangerous... more on that later). The trick, usually, is *not* to try and get them back to your website or blog or book, but just to post a massive info-dump (of crazy useful material) without any links or promotion. In my circle of friends we call this a "Value Bomb."

The point of a Value Bomb is to be insanely helpful without asking for anything in return, by providing well-researched and organized tutorials, case studies, how-to guides, or other useful content. I often share free design templates in big Facebook groups, or tips on how to do book marketing, launch an online course, start a profitable business, or other topics I know a lot about and people are eager to learn. Rather than trying to "sell them" on something or get them back to my site, I just dump and run. I even often say specifically that I *don't* have a course, book, product or any related services, so I'm just doing it to be helpful (this is important especially if you're posting in someone else's groups). If you're trying to be helpful but actually your post is a thinly-veiled indirect attempt at marketing, it'll be seen through quickly (people are smart) and be less effective.

What do I mean by "effective" since I'm not selling anything? On Facebook, people who find your post useful might follow or friend you. You get a reputation of providing great content. I may only post in a big group once every few months, but that one Value Bomb will get tons of engagement, usually comments like "this is why I love this group so much!" That lets the group owners see me as a valuable person to have in the group, because I'm increasing that group's benefits for everyone involved, and gets me lots of visibility. I may post stuff like that when I *also* have something promotional on my Facebook page, so when they see my content, and click on my profile, they'll see whatever thing I'm actually promoting. But not always.

For my last course launch, I shared tips on launching a course, and I shared on my Facebook page that my course was doing really well (enough to pay off all of our debt) but I didn't actually *link* to the course anywhere. People were curious, but couldn't find it. I did add links to some of my other Facebook pages. And I also was spending money boosting really great blog articles that were getting shares, to get people to my blog, where they could also see a post about the course.

Actually I probably need to do less indirect marketing and more direct stuff, which I'll do on my next course launch. It's fine to ask people to buy things. But not usually at the *first point of contact.* You need to get in front of them indirectly by providing value, establishing your credibility and reputation, making people aware of you (and hopefully like you). For non-fiction, you need to show you're an expert. For fiction, you need to get them *actually reading your story*, which is why free books work so well (it's easier to publish a permafree book and do no marketing, than spend money trying to get in front of the same readers on Facebook and offering them a free book to join your email list). Don't be afraid to ask for the sale; but make sure you earn their trust before you do.

COMMUNITY CONTENT

I'll sometimes crowdsource content from my groups or email lists. For example, I asked everyone to take the first 10 italic phrases of their books and put them together to make a little story. It was a cool *snapshot* of their books. Then we put them altogether as a piece of content, that everybody can share. It features our book covers and links, but isn't meant to be promotional.$1000 on Ki

Going for broke
One of the more extravagant ideas I've had for promoting *Shearwater* is creating the site www. TaylorSwiftisReallyaMermaid.com.

It's unfinished, and I don't know if I will actually finish it. But if it's very cool, kind of bizarre, and basically does nothing except direct people to donate money to Greenpeace or other big oceanic conservation sites, it could get lots of traffic quickly. It's the kind of thing that *could* do really well on Reddit, or get viral traffic. I know that Taylor really does love mermaids, so it's mostly a creative T-Swift fanpage. Taylor Swift's audience is basically who I think will also enjoy *Shearwater* (people who love fantasy, mermaids and tragic romances).

I may clean it up some more and see if I can send some traffic to it. Ideally (in my wildest dreams) Taylor Swift would see it and share it; maybe even review my book (her other favorite book is about mermaids). But even if she didn't, if I could get a lot of people who like Taylor Swift + Mermaids to see and share it, I could reach a lot of my target audience. Eventually, when it gets lots of traffic,

I could add a link to my book, or "top 25 best mermaid books" or something with mine at the top.

This is the kind of indirect marketing that can be fun, but normally isn't something I'd recommend. This stuff wouldn't work *by itself*, and lots of authors start off with big ideas like this (getting featured on Oprah) without ever putting the basics into place. Even so, if you hope to get celebs to talk about you, you need to *do something interesting*.

The castle thing

A few years ago I decided I wanted to buy a castle and use it as a writing retreat. I'd still like to. We've been to Europe for three months for the past three years, looking at properties. I can't actually afford one, but if my platform gets big enough I hope to use Kickstarter to raise funds.

But most people think it's just a dream, or that it's impractical, so in 2016 I rented a castle on AirBNB and stayed there for a month, to do Nanowrimo with fifteen other authors. I got a lot of visibility, and even got featured by CNN (not to mention building relationships with the Nanowrimo community). It wasn't easy, and I spent a lot of money to make it happen... but the exposure was worth it.

Now I can say "as featured in CNN" whenever I have something to promote. And being the guy who rents castles to use as writing retreats is good for both my fiction and non-fiction platforms. It's a little crazy and impractical, but it's also something that resonates with people and stands out. There are hundreds of authors in the self-publishing space who constantly promote their sites or services, write great content, organize webinars or online summits. Those things work too. But you need more. You need a mission, and you need to be doing epic things that fire up people's imaginations. I'll probably rent a castle every year from now on – I'm still figuring out how to run profitable events (so I at least break even, rather than spending a lot of my own money), but it's something I can do to build my brand and platform, and get people aware of who I am and the things that I do.

If you want people to talk about you or share your content, it's probably not going to be because of your *book*. That's why I wouldn't send out a press release for a new book I've published. But I will send out a press release about renting a castle for Nanowrimo, because that's news that is likely to catch people's attentions and get shared. You need to find ways to *do* something epic (actually do something, in the real world, something big enough to stand out). It should kind of relate to your platform and the books you want to promote. That said, you don't have to do it right now. For the first year or two, my castle was just an idea, but I still made it a part of my brand. Now we have pictures, and it's a lot more concrete.

In general though, don't get carried away by these big, viral marketing stunts: they aren't going to work unless your book is already making money. Start small with some ads. Once you can consistently get people to buy your book, enjoy it and review it favorably, *then* getting more traffic and visibility will be beneficial. But if you can't sell any books, getting more visibility won't help! Actually, it can hurt: maybe nobody is buying or reviewing your book because the cover is ugly or they didn't enjoy reading it. Doing a huge marketing blitz before you've fixed the problems with your book or Amazon page can lead to negative criticism. Also, doing huge marketing stunts to build awareness may raise expectations, leading to worse reviews. Start small and cheap. $5 a day. Drive some ads. Figure out what's going wrong and fix it.

HOW TO BUILD AN AUTHOR
WEBSITE THAT GETS TRAFFIC

I've decided not to focus on long-term strategies in this book; instead I'll write another book soon about how to build a bestselling author platform in 21 days or less.

But there are still some things I'd like to mention. Firstly, you don't need to constantly be blogging, but you *should* create 10 super articles that attract links and traffic. You can set those up in the first month. Write those articles about the best books in your genre. Write your "favorite passages" from those books as a separate post. Talk about other people to give them a reason to share you (don't just talk about yourself and your own books). Also, talk about things *people are already searching for.*

Personally I like my author websites to be clean and functional, not pretty or fancy. Many authors don't know what people are searching for so they offer *everything* which will get clunky and confusing. You are responsible for organizing a visitor's experience on your site. Don't show them everything. Show them the one thing you actually want them to see. Focus on conversions.

1. Is your website getting any traffic?

2. Is that traffic signing up to your email list or following you?

3. Are they at least buying your book?

If not, your website is a failure, a waste of time and energy, it's useless. Which is why many authors feel frustrated or hate blogging because they don't think it's actually doing anything. It probably isn't. But if you spend a week and fix your website and add some great content, it can work for you on autopilot for years to come. (If you want to see a model of a perfect author website, visit www.authoridentity.com. I'll keep it updated with tips for making an author website that sells and some free templates.

REDISTRIBUTING CONTENT TO WIDEN YOUR FUNNEL

That said, just putting content on your blog isn't likely to be successful, because you're competing with thousands (or millions) of other sites. You need *your* content to show up in search results for keywords before anybody else's site shows up. That may seem daunting, but the good news is, most authors don't know anything about blogging or SEO. So it's actually not that difficult to outrank everyone else, if you try to. The secret is getting lots of backlinks from authority domains. If you want to check your website authority, you can use this Seo Review Tools.

It's also a good idea to check domain authority before committing to any promotions (sometimes the value of a paid promotion can be just getting some links from an authority website). Try to find other authors in your genre with great site authority and see if they'll post something about your book, linking to your site, if you do the same. You're trying to create a "web" of sites that are all talking about your topic or genre, so it's easier for Google to find. You want lots of links back to your site or article, which will increase search results.

I do this by repurposing content. For example, I may write a really in-depth article about a specific cover design trick you can use to sell more books. I'll share that article on Facebook and Twitter, and maybe do some boosted posts. Then I'll make a PowerPoint presentation I can add to SlideShare. Then I'll make a screen record video showing that PowerPoint presentation, or just a "talking head" video discussing the topic, and I'll put those on YouTube. If it's a *central* piece of content, and my best work, I may also put it into my email autoresponder, so everyone who signs up to one of my lists will get to see it.

I should be better about this, especially on YouTube: rather than having dozens of videos on a topic, I should have one amazing video I send everybody to, which will mean more views, so that YouTube will start sharing it more.

My point is, don't just keep creating new content without promoting it. Use that same content and repurpose it, by turning it into different formats and putting it up on lots of different sites. Organize your links so you have some nice keyword links to your main piece of content, or your book on Amazon. Focus on building 5 or 10 amazing pieces of content that get lots of views and shares; the more links you can get to it, the more it will show up in search results, bringing new traffic to your blog.

You can also reach out to blogs in your community and see if they'll publish a guest post, or if you can write some content for them. Especially for really large websites or blogs, like Huffington Post, this can be worthwhile. Guest posting is powerful: I don't do it much because I'm lazy and I hate asking for permission or following rules and directions. But now that I have lots of <u>friends in the self-publishing industry</u>, I'll probably focus on getting some more articles published on their sites to boost my SEO and traffic.

THE 5 SITES YOU NEED TO BE USING (AND HOW TO PUT CONTENT ON THEM QUICKLY THAT WILL BRING YOU SALES FOR YEARS TO COME)

Here are my favorite sites. I don't actually use them all as much as I should, but they're important to know.

Goodreads is a huge book related site where readers can talk about books. It's a *social* site, not a promotional site. And reviewers can tend to be harsher, so generally I don't spend much time on it. But Goodreads has a section where you can add your books to lists, and those list pages show up really well in Google search results. So if you Google "best science fiction books" or anything like that, you'll probably see a Goodreads list on the first page. That's a list you should try to get on. You can add your own books to lists, and if your followers like them, they can vote your book up higher. I wouldn't try to game the system or push your book up too high; I generally try to be in the top 100 books in those lists. I don't manage my Goodreads profile or page well at all (it's a mess) but my books are there and I know they're getting seen. Once I have full series out and am making a lot more money with my fiction, tweaking Goodreads more could make a big impact. (You can also make print book giveaways on Goodreads which is a simple way to get more visibility and get your book added to some "to be read" lists.)

Reddit is one of the biggest sites on the internet, and can send a ton of traffic to your blog or book. But it can be dangerous. Reddit users are anonymous, and they tend to be critical. Anything that's promotional will not do well. People can upvote your content, and you want great content that gets more visibility. There are sections for free or discount books though, so you can post your promotion there; however I'd still try to make it engaging and authentic (be human, ask them what they think... treat other people like you care about their opinion, don't just dump your link and run).

Reddit can also be great for sharing excellent content and getting more traffic, but usually not for just posting links to your own blog or website. It's a tricky platform, so it's best to join some groups and watch what kind of things do well, and aim to make something similar. Learn the rules before you start posting. But don't worry if your first few (dozen) posts bomb. If you figure it out and get something to the top of Reddit it can get millions of views. On Reddit is where you'll want to try your indirect marketing: don't promote your book, so much as share interesting content that potential readers of your book will enjoy.

YouTube. Even if your videos don't get tons of views, they may still show up well in search results and the links from YouTube to your book or content might help your SEO. For example, I really should have made a PowerPoint or video about my "best young adult mermaid books" post and added that to YouTube. It's not a very competitive keyword string, so it's likely a YouTube video will show up on the first page of Google; then in the description I can add a link back to the full article, which has links to all the books.

Most fiction authors aren't using YouTube at all; while there are a many BookTubers (people who review books on YouTube) these are mostly for young adult literature, and there's a lot of space for doing things differently around keywords related to your book or topics. If you don't feel comfortable on camera (I hated it for the first year) you can just record your screen and talk about things. I've also considered hiring someone to read my book out loud in a video series... something I may try to do soon.

SlideShare is interesting for me, because for a lot of my videos or courses I need to make a PowerPoint anyway (actually, I'm not a fan of PowerPoint, I've been using Google Slides instead.) So I can just upload my slides and add some links (you can add links inside your slides, too). SlideShare is owned by LinkedIn, another powerful site, more geared towards business networking. Especially for non-fiction, if you have a great presentation on a cool topic, SlideShare and LinkedIn might share it with their followers. Even if not, you can get some powerful links back to your content. I don't use LinkedIn much but you can also be active in their forums, or use "Pulse" to publish your content on their platform. Once you've figured out what your main pieces of content are going to be, try and put versions of it everywhere (not the exact same thing, but an altered version or parallel topic so you can link to it).

Pinterest

Stop the press. I have less than 24 hours to finish, edit, format and upload this book, but I just stopped writing for an hour because I had an idea so good I had to go start doing it right away... so that I can tell you about it. (As long as I do it first, I don't mind sharing).

I was going to say, Pinterest is a major website and images perform really well. So you should be focused on making graphics. Book promotion or covers won't work that well, but image quotes (a picture where the text is written against a pretty background) do very well. So you can make image quotes using the best passages from your books; you can do the same thing with best passages from other bestselling books in your genre, or other authors you'd like to support. You put all those together on a nice blog post (or somewhere you can post content) with all those images, and easy buttons for sharing. Then you also pin them on Pinterest. Every day you can post an image quote to Twitter, Facebook and Instagram.

Use some art, possibly the book cover, a nicely designed quote and in small text the name of the author. Share those. For the really big, bestselling authors, you can *boost* those Tweets or Facebook posts to people who like those authors. They are very likely to share or retweet it. Having your content shared will bring you more followers and more traffic. That's such a good idea, I need to start doing it myself. So I just emailed my assistant to have her start working on it. But actually, finding all those quotes is slow and will be hard work. So I decided to just email my lists and ask them to send in favorite quotes from their favorite books. I can set up a Facebook post asking for quotes, they can either write out the quote or take a picture and upload it, and my assistant can go through and collect all the quotes so we can start making graphics.

But *also*, I can turn it into a contest to get more engagement. So I'll offer $20 in Amazon credit to each of the ten best quotes (and maybe one $100 big prize for the best quote ever). This will make it more of a game, a scavenger hunt, where people will spend some time looking and uploading quotes for us to use. It'll be *fun,* and get lots of shares and engagement, which will bring in new likes and followers (rather than just building the content to gain traffic, I can use the *process* of gathering the data to gain traffic).

I can take it a step *further* by collecting the quotes, turning the top contenders into image quotes, and then asking everybody to vote on their favorites (I'd have to keep track of who submitted each quote but as long as we stay on Facebook it'd be pretty easy). So that's potentially a few months of great content that will build my platform, just to *make* some good content that will build my platform.

ANTHOLOGIES AND BOXSETS

Recently I've been involved in two big multi-author projects. First, I organized an anthology of young adult fiction for my Facebook group (The Alliance of YA Authors). We decided to publish it as permafree – it's basically just for visibility. The benefit is, it's really easy for 42 authors promoting a book together to get that book to the top of Amazon.

I did all the formatting and design, set up the Kindle and print books, and then published with Draft2Digital to get Kindle to price-match it. (If I didn't mention it earlier, that's how to publish a permafree book – you tell Amazon about the cheaper price and ask support to price match it to free).

For promotion, I made a big post on my fiction blog here, with all the links and a link to all of the authors' websites – then I shared the html code so they could repost (they should edit and rearrange, not post identical content... but, having us all link to each other's sites and having lots of keyword-anchored links to the book on Amazon is great for long term visibility.)

With all the links from our sites, and with us all sharing to our lists, we can get it pretty high and it will probably stick there. 1000 downloads gets us into the top 100.

10,000 downloads might get us to #1 – which is my goal, but if we get into the top 10, that would be great too. However... getting up to the top of Amazon isn't all it's cracked up to be. You'll get a lot of freebie seekers who aren't your target audience, and they might review it badly.

You really want to be up at the top of your category (for us, "young adult") but not much higher. Update: we just barely cracked the top 100, but since then (over a month later) we're still in the top #2000 free, and #1 in *young adult > short stories*. Especially for those authors who don't have a permafree book already as part of their funnel, it should be good for a lot of visibility.

The other project I've joined is a boxset of 20 authors that a friend of mine organized. The boxset is called "Dark Legends" and it's a great fit for my book *Orpheum* which is based on Greek Mythology.

In this case, all the authors pitched in advertising money. With a paid book, even with lots of promotion, it's hard to keep getting consistent daily sales. (After we all share the book to our own audience, we need to keep finding ways to reach new buyers). I try to reach new readers with natural traffic or advertising. The goal of boxsets like this is usually to hit the big bestseller's lists: both the USA Today and the NYT bestseller lists allow for ebook boxsets, and so when authors team up like this it's not too difficult (or at least much easier) to hit the lists.

That can take a huge advertising budget, so I don't usually recommend it. But even so, boxsets are a fun way to partner with other authors, and bring people together as part of a team, and use all of that effort to reach lots of new readers.

You can do a lot of good just by being the one who tries to put something like this together, however it can be hard to get people to trust you if they don't know you. Firstly, I'd write some posts about the best indie books in your genre and let authors know about it; and also review their books; and follow them and interact with them online. Participate in genre-specific book groups and forums. This doesn't have to be intense or take up a lot of time, but you do need to be a little visible. Also if you post an invitation to join your boxset or anthology, you should have enough experience publishing to put together something of good quality.

That said, everybody has to start somewhere. Try it out, see if you get any takers, form a group, get help. See how it goes. My main point is, often it's much easier to market a book as a team and get much bigger results, which is good for everyone involved.

★ If this seems daunting, an easier thing to do is run an Instafreebie giveaway. Find 20 or so books in your genre on Instafreebie, or put out calls in groups to find other authors who have books in Instafreebie. Make one big blog post on your site with all the book covers, descriptions and links to the free book on Instafreebie. Get all the authors to share and promote it (sending all their followers to *your* site). If you tell Instafreebie about your promotion they might share it with their lists also. All that traffic can click on the free books they want and sign up for that author's newsletter. This can be really powerful for list-building.

★ Not sure if I mentioned earlier, but you can give away ARC copies of the book on Instafreebie before launch; if you're in KDP Select you can't keep giving out the free book, but you could make an altered version, maybe with just the first 30% of the book and a link to get the full book on Amazon.

WHAT'S NEXT

STOP MARKETING AND WRITE MORE BOOKS!

Writing more books isn't a solution if you don't have an online platform that attracts readers, or if your basics (cover design, reviews, description) aren't getting any sales. But long-term, continued marketing is also a waste of time. You need to set up a funnel that attracts and converts readers. You should set that up *now*. But don't spend more than a few weeks on it. Then get back to writing.

TAKE ACTION!

It's great to learn new things, but the majority of authors keep trying to consume more knowledge without actually implementing and seeing results. I don't want that to happen to you. So don't put this book down until you've completed the challenges I've set up. I know that accountability, productivity and motivation are huge problem areas for authors and we need to work together to keep each other on task.

One of the authors in my Facebook group said recently, "I feel like I'm building a 5000 piece jigsaw puzzle on sand." That's because there are huge shifts in the publishing industry. KU might have been great last year, but the fall of 2016 was disastrous for many authors, as page reads plummeted due (probably) to Amazon's new page flip feature. Some of the tools or resources I'm recommending right now (at the beginning of 2016) might not work a year from now. That's why I really want to get you active in my Guerrilla Publishing Facebook group – that way you can stay up to date on new publishing and book marketing developments. But I'm also posting a couple of offers below to help you take action.

This book may feel overwhelming, if you're not used to the intricacies of Kindle publishing or book promotion. Plus, even if you are prepared to dig in and use these tactics, it may take you a long time to figure out all of the technical aspects of setting up an author platform. So I want you to take my free **5-Day Guerrilla Publishing Challenge**. That way I can support you as you focus on taking action now. Every day we'll focus on just one easy-to-do thing you can do in less than 15 minutes, which will help you build a solid platform and see a boost in your sales rank.

NEED MORE HELP?

In this book I mentioned my first course, *Reach Your Readers*, and my next course, *The 21-Day Bestselling Author Platform*. When I launch the companion course to this book, *Guerrilla Publishing*, I'll include both of my other courses for free, along with some other bonuses and resources that will help you publish successfully. But spaces will be limited, and the offer will only be for people who join the 5-Day Challenge. **Sign up so you don't miss out!**

www.creativindie.com/GP

Made in the USA
Columbia, SC
29 May 2018